The slide rule: a practical manual

Charles Newton Pickworth

This work has been selected by scholars as being culturally important, and is part of the knowledge base of civilization as we know it. This work was reproduced from the original artifact, and remains as true to the original work as possible. Therefore, you will see the original copyright references, library stamps (as most of these works have been housed in our most important libraries around the world), and other notations in the work.

This work is in the public domain in the United States of America, and possibly other nations. Within the United States, you may freely copy and distribute this work, as no entity (individual or corporate) has a copyright on the body of the work.

As a reproduction of a historical artifact, this work may contain missing or blurred pages, poor pictures, errant marks, etc. Scholars believe, and we concur, that this work is important enough to be preserved, reproduced, and made generally available to the public. We appreciate your support of the preservation process, and thank you for being an important part of keeping this knowledge alive and relevant.

THE SLIDE RULE

BY THE SAME AUTHOR.

LOGARITHMS FOR BEGINNERS.

"An extremely useful and much-needed little work, giving a complete explanation of the theory and use of logarithms, by a teacher of great clearness and good style."—*The Mining Journal.*

1s. 8d. Post Free.

THE INDICATOR HANDBOOK.

Comprising "The Indicator: Its Construction and Application" and "The Indicator Diagram: Its Analysis and Calculation." Complete in One Volume.

7s. 10d. Post Free.

"Mr Pickworth's judgment is always sound, and is evidently derived from a personal acquaintance with indicator work."—*The Engineer.*

POWER COMPUTER
FOR STEAM, GAS AND OIL ENGINES, Etc.

"Accurate, expeditious and thoroughly practical... We can confidently recommend it, and engineers will find it a great boon in undertaking tests, etc."—*The Electrician.*

7s. 6d. Post Free.

C. N. PICKWORTH, WITHINGTON, MANCHESTER.

THE SLIDE RULE:

A PRACTICAL MANUAL

BY

CHARLES N. PICKWORTH

WHITWORTH SCHOLAR; EDITOR OF "THE MECHANICAL WORLD"; AUTHOR OF
"LOGARITHMS FOR BEGINNERS"; "THE INDICATOR: ITS CONSTRUCTION
AND APPLICATION"; "THE INDICATOR DIAGRAM: ITS ANALYSIS AND
CALCULATION," ETC.

SEVENTEENTH EDITION

MANCHESTER:
EMMOTT AND CO., LIMITED,
65 KING STREET;

NEW YORK:
D. VAN NOSTRAND CO.,
8 WARREN STREET

LONDON:
EMMOTT AND CO., LIMITED,
20 BEDFORD STREET, W.C.

AND

PITMAN AND SONS, LIMITED,
PARKER ST., KINGSWAY, W.C. 2.

[*Three Shillings and Sixpence net*]

All rights reserved.

PREFACE TO THE FIFTEENTH EDITION.

SEVERAL new slide rules for special calculations are described in this edition, and the contents further extended to include a section dealing with screw-cutting gear calculations by the slide rule—an application of the instrument to which attention has been given recently.

Mention should be made of the fact that some of the special slide rules described in previous editions are no longer obtainable. As, however, the descriptive notes may be of service to those possessing the instruments, and are, in some measure, of general interest, they have been allowed to remain in the present issue.

The author tenders his thanks to the many who have evinced their appreciation of his efforts to popularise the subject; also for the many kind hints and suggestions which he has received from time to time, and with a continuance of which he trusts to be favoured in the future.

C. N. P.

WITHINGTON, MANCHESTER, *November* 1917.

PREFACE TO THE SEVENTEENTH EDITION.

THE sustained demand for this very successful work having resulted in the early call for a new edition, the opportunity has been taken to introduce descriptions of new slide rules and to effect some slight revisions.

C. N. P.

WITHINGTON, MANCHESTER, *December* 1920.

CONTENTS.

	PAGE
Introductory	5
The Mathematical Principle of the Slide Rule	6
Notation by Powers of 10	8
The Mechanical Principle of the Slide Rule	9
The Primitive Slide Rule	10
The Modern Slide Rule	12
The Notation of the Slide Rule	14
The Cursor or Runner	17
Multiplication	19
Division	24
The Use of the Upper Scales for Multiplication and Division	26
Reciprocals	27
Continued Multiplication and Division	28
Multiplication and Division with the Slide Inverted	30
Proportion	31
General Hints on the Elementary Uses of the Slide Rule	36
Squares and Square Roots	37
Cubes and Cube Roots	40
Miscellaneous Powers and Roots	45
Powers and Roots by Logarithms	45
Other Methods of Obtaining Powers and Roots	47
Combined Operations	49
Hints on Evaluating Expressions	52
Gauge Points	53
Examples in Technical Calculations	56
Trigonometrical Application	74
Slide Rules with Log-log Scales	84
Special Types of Slide Rules	92
Long Scale Slide Rules	96
Circular Calculators	101
Slide Rules for Special Calculations	109
Constructional Improvements in Slide Rules	110
The Accuracy of Slide Rule Results	111
Appendix:—	
New Slide Rules	113
The Solution of Algebraic Equations	122
Screw-Cutting Gear Calculations	124
Gauge Points and Signs on Slide Rules	126
Tables and Data	128
Slide Rule Data Slips	133

THE SLIDE RULE.

INTRODUCTORY.

THE slide rule may be defined as an instrument for mechanically effecting calculations by logarithms. Those familiar with logarithms and their use will recognise that the slide rule provides what is in effect a concisely arranged table of logarithms, together with a simple and convenient means for adding and subtracting any selected values. Those, however, who have no acquaintance with logarithms will find that only an elementary knowledge of the subject is necessary to enable them to make full use of the slide rule. It is true that for simple slide-rule operations, as multiplication and division, a knowledge of logarithms is unnecessary; indeed, many who have no conscious understanding of logarithms make good use of the instrument. But this involves a blind reliance upon rules without an appreciation of their origin or limitations, and this, in turn, engenders a want of confidence in the results of any but the simplest operations, and prevents the fullest use being made of the instrument. For this reason a brief, but probably sufficient *résumé* of the principles of logarithmic calculation will be given. Those desiring a more detailed explanation are referred to the writer's "Logarithms for Beginners."

The slide rule enables various arithmetical, algebraical and trigonometrical processes to be performed with ease and rapidity, and with sufficient accuracy for most practical purposes. A grasp of the simple fundamental principles which underlie its operation, together with a little patient practice, are all that are necessary to acquire facility in using the instrument, and few who have become proficient in this system of calculating would willingly revert to the laborious arithmetical processes.

THE MATHEMATICAL PRINCIPLE OF THE SLIDE RULE.

LOGARITHMS may be defined as a series of numbers in *arithmetical* progression, as 0, 1, 2, 3, 4, etc., which bear a definite relationship to another series of numbers in *geometrical* progression, as 1, 2, 4, 8, 16, etc. A more precise definition is:—The logarithm of a number to any base, is the *index of the power* to which the base must be raised to equal the given number. In the logarithms in general use, known as *common logarithms*, and with which we are alone concerned, 10 is the base selected. The general definition may therefore be stated in the following modified form:—*The common logarithm of a number is the index of the power to which 10 must be raised to equal the given number.* Applying this rule to a simple case, as $100 = 10^2$, we see that the base 10 must be squared (*i.e.*, raised to the 2nd power) in order to equal 100, the number selected. Therefore, as 2 is the index of the power to which 10 must be raised to equal 100, it follows from our definition that 2 is the common logarithm of 100. Similarly the common logarithm of 1000 will be 3, while proceeding in the opposite direction the common log. of 10 must equal 1. Tabulating these results and extending, we have:—

Numbers	10,000	1000	100	10	1
Logarithms	4	3	2	1	0

It will now be evident that for numbers

between	1 and	10	the logs. will be between	0 and	1
,,	10 ,,	100	,, ,,	1 ,,	2
,,	100 ,,	1000	,, ,,	2 ,,	3
,,	1000 ,,	10,000	,, ,,	3 ,,	4

In other words, the logarithms of numbers between 1 and 10 will be wholly fractional (*i.e.*, decimal); the logs. of numbers between 10 and 100 will be 1 *followed by a decimal quantity;* the logs. of numbers between 100 and 1000 will be 2 followed by a decimal quantity, and so on. These decimal quantities for numbers from 1 to 10 (which are the logarithms of this particular series) are as follows:—

Numbers	1	2	3	4	5	6	7	8	9	10
Logarithms	0	0·301	0·477	0·602	0·699	0·778	0·845	0·903	0·954	1·000

Combining the two tables, we can complete the logarithms. Thus for 3 multiplied successively by 10, we have:—

Numbers	3	30	300	3000	30,000	etc.
Logarithms	0·477	1·477	2·477	3·477	4·477	

We see from this that for numbers having the *same significant figure* (or figures), 3 in this case, the decimal part or *mantissa* of the logarithm is the same, but that the integral part or *characteristic* is always *one less than the number of figures before the decimal point*.

For numbers less than 1 the same plan is followed. Thus extending our first table downwards, we have:—

Numbers	1	0·1	0·01	0·001	0·0001	etc.
Logarithms	0	−1	−2	−3	−4	

so that for 3 divided successively by 10, we have:—

Numbers	3	0·3	0·03	0·003	0·0003	etc.
Logarithms	0·477	$\bar{1}$·477	$\bar{2}$·477	$\bar{3}$·477	$\bar{4}$·477	

Here again we see that with the same significant figures in the numbers, the mantissa of the logarithm has always the same (*positive*) value, but the characteristic is *one more* than the *number of 0's immediately following the decimal point*, and is *negative*, as indicated by the minus sign written over it. Only the decimal parts of the logarithms of numbers between 1 and 10 are given in the usual tables, for, as shown above, the logarithms of all tenfold multiples or submultiples of a number can be obtained at once by modifying the characteristic in accordance with the rules given.

An examination of the two rows of figures giving the logarithms of numbers from 1 to 10 will reveal some striking peculiarities, and at the same time serve to illustrate the principle of logarithmic calculation. First, it will be noticed that the addition of any two of the logarithms gives the logarithm of the *product* of these two numbers. Thus, the addition of log. 2 and log. 4 = 0·301 + 0·602 = 0·903, and this is seen to be the logarithm of 8, that is, of 2 × 4. Conversely, the difference of the logarithms of two numbers gives the logarithm of the *quotient* resulting from the division of these two numbers. Thus, log. 8 − log. 2 = 0·903 − 0·301 = 0·602, which is the log. of 4, or of 8 ÷ 2.

One other important point is to be noted. If the logarithm of any number is *multiplied* by 2, 3, or any other quantity, whole or fractional, the result is the logarithm of the original number, raised to the 2nd, 3rd, or other power respectively. Thus, multiplying the log. of 3 by 2, we obtain $0.477 \times 2 = 0.954$, and this is seen to be the log. of 9, that is, of 3 raised to the 2nd power, or 3 *squared*. Again, log. 2 multiplied by $3 = 0.903$—that is, the log. of 8, or of 2 raised to the 3rd power, or 2 *cubed*. Conversely, dividing the logarithm of any original number by any number n, we obtain the logarithm of the nth root of the original number. Thus, log. $8 \div 3 = 0.903 \div 3 = 0.301$, and is therefore equal to log. 2 or to the log. of the *cube root* of 8.

Only simple logs. have been taken in these examples, but the student will understand that the same reasoning applies, whatever the number. Thus for 20^3 we prefix the characteristic (1 in this case) to log. 2, giving 1.301. Multiplying by 3, we have 3.903 as the resulting logarithm, and as its characteristic is 3, we know that it corresponds to the number 8000. Hence $20^3 = 8000$.

In this brief explanation is included all that need now be said with regard to the properties of logarithms. The main facts to be borne clearly in mind are:—(1.) That to find the *product* of two numbers, the logarithms of the numbers are to be *added* together, the result being the logarithm of the product required, the value of which can then be determined. (2.) That in finding the *quotient* resulting from the division of one number by another, *the difference* of the logarithms of the numbers gives the logarithm of the quotient, from which the value of the latter can be ascertained. (3.) That to find the result of *raising a number to the nth power*, we *multiply* the logarithm of the number by n, thus obtaining the logarithm, and hence the value, of the desired result. And (4.) That to find the nth *root of a number*, we *divide* the logarithm of the number by n, this giving the logarithm of the result, from which its value may be determined.

NOTATION BY POWERS OF 10.

A CONVENIENT method of representing an arithmetical quantity is to split it up into two factors, of which the first is the original number, with the decimal point moved so as to immediately follow the first significant figure, and the second, 10^n where n is the number of places the decimal point has been moved, this index being *positive* for numbers greater than 1, and *negative* for numbers less than 1.* In this system, therefore, we regard 3,610,000 as $3.61 \times 1,000,000$, and write it as 3.61×10^6. Similarly $361 = 3.61 \times 10^2$; $0.0361 \left(= \dfrac{3.61}{100}\right) = 3.61 \times 10^{-2}$; $0.0000361 = 3.61 \times 10^{-5}$, etc. To restore a number to its original form, we have only to move the decimal point through the number of places indicated by the index, moving to the right if the index is positive and to the left (prefixing 0's) if negative. This method, which should be cultivated for ordinary arithmetical work, is substantially that followed in calculating by the slide rule. Thus with the slide rule the multiplication of 63,200 by 0.0035 virtually resolves itself into $6.32 \times 10^4 \times 3.5 \times 10^{-3}$ or $6.32 \times 3.5 \times 10^{4-3} = 22.12 \times 10^1 = 221.2$. It will be seen later, however, that the result can be arrived at by a more direct, if less systematic, method of working.

THE MECHANICAL PRINCIPLE OF THE SLIDE RULE.

The mechanical principle involved in the slide rule is of a very simple character. In Fig. 1, A and B represent two rules divided into 10 equal parts, the division lines being numbered consecutively

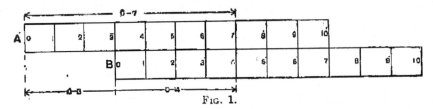

Fig. 1.

as shown. If the rule B is moved to the right until 0 on B is opposite 3 on A, it is seen that any number on A is equal to the coinciding number on B, plus 3. Thus opposite 4 on B is 7 on A. The reason is obvious. By moving B to the right, we add to a length 0-3, another length 0-4, the result read off on A being 7. Evidently, the same result would have been obtained if a length 0-4 had been added, by means of a pair of dividers, to the length 0-3 on the scale A. By means of the slide B, however, the addition is more readily effected, and, what is of much greater importance,

---

* It will be recognised that n is the characteristic of the logarithm of the original number.

the result of adding 3 to *any one of the numbers* within range, on the lower scale, is *immediately* seen by reading the adjacent number on A.

Of course, subtraction can be quite as readily performed. Thus, to subtract 4 from 7, we require to deduct from 0-7 on the A scale, a length 0-4 on B. We do this by placing 4 on B under 7 on A, when over 0 on B we find 3, on A. It is here evident that the *difference* of any pair of coinciding numbers on the scales is constantly equal to 3.

An important modification results if the slide-scale B is inverted as in Fig. 2. In this case, to find the sum of 4 and 3 we require to place the 4 of the A scale to 3 on the B scale, and the result is read on A over 0 on B. Here it will be noted, the *sum* of any pair of coinciding numbers on the scales is constant and

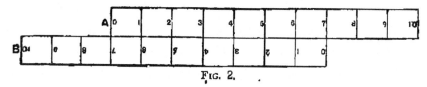

Fig. 2.

equal to 7. This case, therefore, resembles that of the immediately preceding one, except that the *sum*, instead of the *difference*, of any pair of coinciding numbers is constant

To find the difference of two factors, the converse operation is necessary. Thus, to subtract 4 from 7, 0 on B is placed opposite 7 on A, and over 4 on B is found 3 on A.

From these examples it will be seen that with the slide *inverted* the methods of operation are the reverse of those used when the slide is in its normal position.

It will be understood that although we have only considered the primary divisions of the scales, the remarks apply equally to any subdivisions into which the primary spaces of the scales might be divided. Further, we note that the length of scale taken to represent a unit is quite arbitrary.

THE PRIMITIVE SLIDE RULE.

The application of the foregoing principles to the slide rule can be shown most conveniently by describing the construction of a simple form of slide rule:—Take a strip of card about 11in. long and 2in. wide; draw a line down the centre of its width, and mark off two points, 10in. apart. Draw cross lines at these points and figure them 1 and 10 on each side, as in Fig. 3. Next mark off lengths of 3·01, 4·77, 6·02, 6·99, 7·78, 8·45, 9·03 and 9·54 inches, from the line marked 1. Draw cross lines as before, and figure these lines, 2, 3, 4, 5, 6, 7, 8 and 9. To fill in the intermediate divisions of the scale, take the logs. of 1·1, 1·2, 1·3, etc. (from a table), multiply each by 10, and thus obtain the distances from 1,

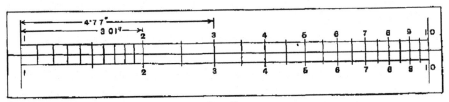

FIG. 3.

at which the several subdivisions are to be placed. Mark these 1·2, 1·3, 1·4, etc., and complete the scale, making the interpolated division marks shorter to facilitate reading, as with an ordinary measuring rule. Cutting the card cleanly down the centre line, we have the essentials of the slide rule.

The fundamental principle of the slide rule is now evident:—Each scale is graduated in such a manner that the *distance of any number from 1 is proportional to the logarithm of that number.*

We know that to find the product of 2 × 3 by logarithms, we add 0·301, or log. 2, to 0·477, the log. of 3, obtaining 0·778, or log. 6. With our primitive slide rule we place 1 on the lower scale to

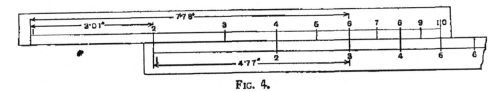

FIG. 4.

3·01in. (which we have marked 2) on the upper scale (Fig. 4). Then over 4·77in. on the lower scale (which we marked 3), we have 7·78in. (which we marked 6) on the upper scale. Conversely, to divide 6 by 3, we place 3 on the lower scale in agreement with 6 on the upper, and over 1 on the lower scale read 2 on the upper scale. This method of adding and subtracting scale lengths will be seen to be identical with that used in the simple case shown in Fig. 1.

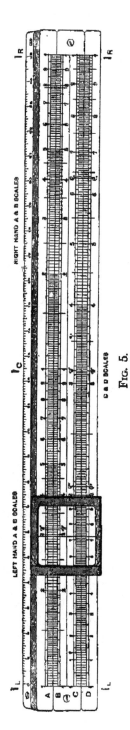

Fig. 5.

THE MODERN SLIDE RULE.

The modern form of slide rule, variously styled the Gravêt, the Tavernier-Gravêt, and the Mannheim rule, is frequently made of boxwood, but all the leading instrument makers now supply rules made of boxwood or mahogany, and faced with celluloid, the white surface of which brings out the graduations much more distinctly than lines engraved on a boxwood surface. The celluloid facings should not be polished, as a dull surface is much less fatiguing to the eyes. The most generally used, and on the whole the most convenient size of rule, is about 10½in. long, 1¼in. wide, and about ⅜in. thick; but 5in., 8in., 15in., 20in., 24in. and 40in. rules are also made. In the centre of the stock of the rule a movable slip is fitted, which constitutes the slide, and corresponds to the lower of the two rules of our rudimentary examples.

From Fig. 5, which is a representation of the face of a Gravêt or Mannheim slide rule, it will be seen that four series of logarithmic graduations or scale-lines are employed, the upper and lower being engraved on the stock or body of the rule, while the other two are engraved upon the slide. The two upper sets of graduations are exactly alike in every particular, and the lower sets are also similar. It is usual to identify the two upper scale-lines by the letters A and B, and the two lower by the letters C and D, as indicated in the figure at the left-hand extremities of the scales.

Referring to the scales C and D, these will each be seen to be a development of the elementary scales of Fig. 3, but in this case each principal space is subdivided, more or less minutely. The principle, however, is exactly the same, so that by moving the slide (carrying scale C), multiplication and division can be mechanically performed in the manner described.

The upper scale-line A consists of two exactly similar scales, placed end to end, the first lying between I_L and I_C, and the second between I_C and I_R. The first of these scales will be designated the *left-hand A scale*, and the second the *right-hand A scale*. Similarly the coinciding scales on the slide are the *left-hand B scale* and the *right-hand B scale*. Each of these four scales is divided (as finely as convenient) as in the case of the C and D scales, but, of course, they are exactly one half the length of the latter.

The two end graduations of both the C and D scales are known as the *left-* and *right-hand indices* of these scales. Sometimes they are figured 1 and 10 respectively; sometimes both are marked 1. Similarly I_L and I_R are the left- and right-hand indices of the A and B lines, while I_C is the centre index of these scales. Other division lines usually found on the face of the rule are one on the left-hand A and B scales, indicating the ratio of the circumference of a circle to its diameter, $\pi = 3\cdot1416$; and a line on the right-hand B scale marking the position of $\frac{\pi}{4} = 0\cdot7854$, used in calculating the areas of circles. Reference will be made hereafter to the scales on the under-side of the slide, and we need now only add that one of the edges of the rule, usually bevelled, is generally graduated in millimetres, while the other edge has engraved on it a scale of inches divided into eighths or tenths. On the bottom face inside the groove of the rule either one or the other of these scales is continued in such a manner that by drawing the slide out to the right and using the scale inside the rule, in conjunction with the corresponding scale on the edge, it is possible to measure 20 inches in the one case, or nearly 500 millimetres in the other. On the back of the rule there is usually a collection of data, for which the slips given at the end of this work may often be substituted with advantage.

THE NOTATION OF THE SLIDE RULE.

HITHERTO our attention has been confined to a consideration of the primary divisions of the scales. The same principle of graduation is, however, used throughout; and after what has been said, this part of the subject need not be further enlarged upon. Some explanation of the method of reading the scales is necessary, as facility in using the instrument depends in a very great measure upon the dexterity of the operator in assigning the correct value to each division on the rule. By reference to Fig. 5, it will be seen that each of the primary spacings in the several scales is invariably subdivided into ten; but since the lengths of the successive primary divisions rapidly diminish, it is impossible to subdivide each main space into the same number of parts that the space 1-2 can be subdivided. This variable spacing of the scales is at first confusing to the student, but with a little practice the difficulty is soon overcome.

With the C or D scale, it will be noticed that the length of the interval 1-2 is sufficient to allow each of the 10 subdivisions to be again divided into 10 parts, so that the whole interval 1-2 is divided into 100. The shorter main space 2-3, and the still shorter one 3-4, only allow of the 10 subdivisions of each being divided into five parts. Each of these main spaces is therefore divided into 50 parts. For the remainder of the scale each of the 10 subdivisions of each main space is divided into two parts only; so that from the main division 4 to the end of the scale the primary spaces are divided into 20 parts only.

In the upper scales A or B, it will be found that—as the space 1-2 is of only half the length of the corresponding space on C or D—the 10 subdivisions of this interval are divided into five parts only. Similarly each of the 10 subdivisions of the intervals 2-3, 3-4, and 4-5 are further divided into two parts only, while for the remainder of the scale only the 10 subdivisions are possible, owing to the rapidly diminishing lengths of the primary spacings.

The values actually given on the rule run from 1 to 10 on the lower scales and from 1 to 100 on the upper scales, and, as explained on page 9, all factors are brought within these ranges of values by multiplying or dividing them by powers of 10. By following this plan, we virtually regard each factor as merely a series of significant figures, and make the necessary modification due to the "powers of 10" when fixing the position of the decimal point in the answer.

Many, however, find it convenient in practice to regard the values on the rule as multiplied or divided by such powers of 10 as may be necessary to suit the factors entering into the calculation. If this plan is adopted, the values given to each graduation of the scales will depend on that given to the left index figure (1) of the lower scales, this being any multiple or submultiple of 10. Thus I_L on the D scale may be regarded as 1, 10, 100, 1000, etc., or as 0·1, 0·01, 0·001, 0·0001, etc.; but once the initial value is assigned to the index, the ratio of value must be maintained throughout the whole scale. For example, if 1 on C is taken to represent 10, the main divisions 2, 3, 4, etc., will be read as 20, 30, 40, etc. On the other hand, if the fourth main division is read as 0·004, then the left index figure of the scale will be read as 0·001. The figured subdivisions of the main space 1-2 are to be read as 11, 12, 13, 14, 15, 16, 17, 18 and 19—if the index represents 10,—and as corresponding multiples for any other value of the index.

Independently considered, these remarks apply equally to the A or B scale, but in this case the notation is continued through the second half of the scale, the figures of which are to be read as tenfold values of the corresponding figures in the first half of the scale.

The reading of the intermediate divisions will, of course, be determined by the values assigned to the main divisions. Thus, if I_L on D is read as 1, then each of the smallest subdivisions of the space 1-2 will be read as 0·01, and each of the smallest subdivisions of the spaces 2-3 or 3-4 as 0·02, while for the remainder of the scale the smallest subdivisions are read as 0·05. In the A or B scale the subdivisions of the space 1-2 of the first half of the scale are (if I_L=1) read as 0·02, 0·04, etc.; for the divisions 2-3, 3-4, and 4-5, the smallest intervals are read as 0·05 of the primary spaces, and from 5 to the centre index of the scale the divisions represent 0·1 of each main interval. Passing the centre index, which is now read as 10, the smallest subdivisions immediately following are read 10·2, 10·4, etc., until 20·0 is reached; then we read 20·5, 21·0, 21·5, 22·0, etc., until the figured main division 5 is reached. The remainder of the scale is read 51, 52, 53, etc., up to 100, the right-hand index.

Further subdivision of any of the spaces of the rule can be effected by the eye, and after a little practice the operator will become quite expert in estimating any intermediate value. It affords good practice to set 1 on C to 1·04, 1·09, etc. on D, and to read the values on D, under 4, 6, 8, etc. on C. As the exact results are easily calculated mentally, the student, by this means, will receive better instruction in estimating intermediate results than can be given by any diagram.

Some rules will be found figured as shown in Fig. 5; in others, the right-hand upper scales are marked 10, 20, 30, etc. Again, others are marked decimally, the lower scales and the left-hand upper scales being figured 1, 1·1, ·1·2, 1·3 . . . . . 2·5, etc. The latter form has advantages from the point of view of the beginner.

The method of reading the A and B scales, just given, applies only when these scales are regarded as altogether independent of the lower pair of scales C and D. Some operators prefer to use the A and B scales, and some the C and D scales, for the ordinary operations of proportion, multiplication, and division. Each method has its advantages, as will be shown, but in the more complex calculations, as involution and evolution, etc., the relation of the upper scales to the lower scales becomes a very important factor.

The distance 1-10 on the upper scales is one-half of the distance 1-10 on the lower scales. Hence any distance from 1, taken on the upper scales, represents *twice the logarithm* which the same distance represents on the lower scales. In other words, the length which represents log. N on D, would represent 2 log. N on A; and, conversely, the length which represents log. N on A, would represent $\frac{\log. N}{2}$ on D.

Now we have seen (page 8) that multiplying the log of a number by 2 gives the log. of the square of the number. Hence, above any number on D we find its *square* on A, or, conversely, below any number on A, we find its *square root* on D. Thus, above 2 we find 4; under 49, we find 7 and so on. Obviously the same relation exists between the B and C scales.

THE CURSOR OR RUNNER.

ALL modern slide rules are now fitted with a *cursor* or *runner*, which usually consists of a light metal frame moving under spring control in grooves in the edges of the stock of the rule. This frame carries a piece of glass, mica or transparent celluloid, about 1in. square, across the centre of which a fine reference line is drawn exactly at right angles to the line of scales. To "set the cursor" to any value on the scales of the rule, the frame is taken between the thumb and forefinger and adjusted in position until the line falls exactly upon the graduation, or upon an estimated value, between a pair of graduations, as the case may be. Having fixed one number in this way, another value on either of the scales on the slide may be similarly adjusted in reference to the cursor line. The cursor will be found very convenient in making such settings, especially when either or both of the numbers are located by eye estimation. It also finds a very important use in referring the readings of the upper scale to those of the lower, or *vice versâ*, while as an aid in continued multiplication and division and complex calculations generally, its value is inestimable.

Multiple Line Cursors.—Cursors can be obtained with *two* lines, the distance between them being that between 7·854 and 10 on the A scale. The use of this cursor is explained on page 57. Another multiple line cursor has short lines engraved on it, corresponding to the main graduations from 95 to 105 on the respective scales. This is useful for adding or deducting small percentages.

The Broken Line Cursor.—To facilitate setting, broken line cursors are made, in which the hair-line is not continued across the scales, but has two gaps, as shown in Fig. 6.

The Pointed Cursor has an index or pointer, extending over the bevelled edge of the rule, on which is a scale of inches. It is useful for summing the lengths of the ordinates of indicator diagrams, and also for plotting lengths representing the logarithms of numbers, sometimes required in graphic calculations.

The Goulding Cursor.—It has been pointed out that in order to obtain the third or fourth figure of a reading on the 10-in. slide rule, it is frequently necessary to depend upon the operator's ability to mentally subdivide the space within which the reading falls. This subdivision can be mechanically effected by the aid of the Goulding Cursor (Fig. 7), which consists of a frame fitting into the usual grooves in the rule, and carrying a metal plate faced with celluloid, upon which is engraved a triangular scale A B C. The portion carrying the chisel edges E is not fixed to the cursor proper, but slides on the latter, so that the index marks on the projecting prongs can be moved slightly along the scales of the rule, this movement being effected by the short end of the bent lever F working in the slot as shown. D is a pointer which can be moved along F under spring control. As illustrating the method of use, we will assume that 1 on C is placed to 155 on D, and that we require to read the value on D under 27 on C. This

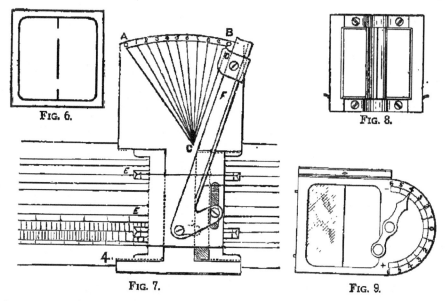

Fig. 6.   Fig. 7.   Fig. 8.   Fig. 9.

is seen to lie between 4150 and 4200, so setting the pointer D to the line B C—always the first operation—we move the whole along the rule until the index line on the lower prong agrees with 4200. We then move F across the scale until the index line agrees with 4100, set the pointer D to the line A C, and move the lever back until the index line agrees with 27 on the slide. It will then be found that the pointer D gives 85 on A B as the value of the supplementary figures, and hence the complete reading is 4185.

Magnifying Cursors are of assistance in reading the scales, and in a good and direct light are very helpful. In one form an ordinary lens is carried by two light arms hinged to the upper and lower edges of the cursor, so that it can be folded down to the face of the rule when not in use. A more compact form, shown in

Fig. 8, consists of a strip of plano-convex glass, on the under side of which is the hair-line. In a cursor made by Nestler of Lahr, the plano-convex strip is fixed on the ordinary cursor. The magnifying power is about 2, so that a 5in. rule, having the same number of graduations as a 10in. rule, can be read with equal facility, by the aid of this cursor.

The Digit-registering Cursor, supplied by Mr A. W. Faber, London, and shown in Fig. 9, has a semicircular scale running from 0 at the centre upward to − 6 and downward to + 6. A small finger enables the operator to register the number of digits to be added or subtracted at the end of a lengthy operation, as explained at page 28.

MULTIPLICATION.

In the preliminary notes it was shown that by mechanically adding two lengths representing the logarithms of two numbers, we can obtain the *product* of these numbers; while by subtracting one

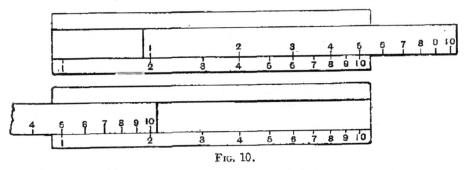

Fig. 10.

log.-length from another, the number represented by the latter is divided by the number represented by the former. Hence, using the C and D scales, we have the

RULE FOR MULTIPLICATION.—*Set the index of the C scale to one of the factors on D, and under the other factor on C, find the product on D.*

Thus, to find the product of 2 × 4, the slide is moved to the right until the left index (1) of C is brought over 2 on D, when under the other factor (4) on C, is found the required product (8) on D. Following along the slide, to the right, we find that beyond 5 on C (giving 10 on D), we have no scale below the projecting slide (Fig. 10). If we imagine the D scale prolonged to the right, we should have a repetition of the earlier portion, but, as with the two parts of the A scales, the repeated portion would be of tenfold value, and 10 on C would agree with 20 on the prolonged D scale. We turn this fact to account by moving the slide to the left until 10 on C agrees with 2 on D, and we can then read off such results as $2 \times 6 = 12$; $2 \times 8 = 16$, etc., remembering that as the scale is now of tenfold value, there will be two figures in the result. Hence, for those who prefer rules, we have the

RULE FOR THE NUMBER OF DIGITS IN A PRODUCT.—*If the product is read with the slide projecting to the* LEFT, ADD THE NUMBER OF THE DIGITS IN THE TWO FACTORS; *if read with the slide to the* RIGHT, *deduct* 1 *from this sum.*

Ex.—$25 \times 70 = 1750$.

The product is found with the slide projecting to the *left*, so the number of digits in the product $= 2 + 2 = 4$.

Ex.—$3 \cdot 6 \times 25 = 90$.

The slide projects to the *right*, and the number of digits in the product is therefore $1 + 2 - 1 = 2$.

Ex.—$0 \cdot 025 \times 0 \cdot 7 = 0 \cdot 0175$.

The product is obtained with the slide projecting to the *left*, and the number of digits is therefore $-1 + 0 = -1$.

Ex.—$0 \cdot 000184 \times 0 \cdot 005 = 0 \cdot 00000092$.

The sum of the number of digits in the two factors $= -3 + (-2) = -5$, but as the slide projects to the *right*, the number of digits will be $-5 - 1 = -6$.

From the last two examples it will be seen that when the first significant figure of a decimal factor does not immediately follow the decimal point, the minus sign is to be prefixed to the number of digits, counting as many digits *minus* as there are 0's following the decimal point. Thus, $0 \cdot 03$ has -1 digit, $0 \cdot 0035$ has -2 digits, and so on. Some little care is necessary to ensure these minus values being correctly taken into account in determining the number of digits in the answer. For this reason many prefer to treat decimal factors as whole numbers, and to locate the decimal point according to the usual rules for the multiplication of decimals. Thus, in the last example we take $184 \times 5 = 920$, but as by the usual rule the product must contain $6 + 3 = 9$ decimal places, we prefix six cyphers, obtaining $0 \cdot 00000092$. When both factors consist of integers as well as decimals, the number of digits in the product, and therefore the position of the decimal point, will be determined by the usual rule for whole numbers.

Another method of determining the number of digits in a product deserves mention, which, not being dependent upon the position of the slide, is applicable to all calculating instruments.

GENERAL RULE FOR NUMBER OF DIGITS IN A PRODUCT.—*When the first significant figure in the product is smaller than in* EITHER *of the factors, the number of digits in the product is equal to the* SUM *of the digits in the two factors. When the contrary is the case, the number of digits is* 1 LESS *than the sum of the digits in the two factors. When the first figures are the same, those following must be compared.*

Estimation of the Figures in a Product.—We have given rules for those who prefer to decide the number of figures by this means, but experience will show that to make the best use of the instrument, the result, as read on the rule, should be regarded merely as the *significant figures of the answer*, the position of the decimal point, if not obvious, being decided by a very rough mental calculation. In very many instances, the magnitude of the result will be evident from the conditions of the problem—*e.g.*, whether the answer should be 0·3in., 3in., or 30in.; or 10 tons, 0·1 ton, 100 tons, etc. In those cases where the magnitude of the answer cannot be estimated, and the factors contain many figures, or have a number of 0's following the decimal point, the use of notation by powers of 10 (page 8) is of considerable assistance; but more usually it will be found that a very rough calculation will settle the point with comparatively little trouble. Considerable practice is needed to work rapidly and with certainty, when using rules. Moreover, the experience thus acquired is confined to slide-rule work. The same time spent in practising the "rough approximation" method will enable reliable results to be obtained rapidly, with the advantage that the method is applicable to calculations generally. However, the choice of methods is a matter of personal preference. Both methods will be given, but whichever plan is followed, the student is strongly advised to cultivate the habit of forming an idea of the magnitude of the result.

Ex.—$33·6 \times 236 = 7930$.

Setting 1 on C to 33·6 on D, we read under 236 on D and find 793 on D, as the significant figures of the answer. A rough calculation, as $30 \times 200 = 6000$, indicates that the result will consist of 4 figures, and is therefore to be read as 7930.

Ex.—17,300 × 3780 = 65,400,000.

By factorising with powers of 10

$1{\cdot}73 \times 10^4 \times 3{\cdot}78 \times 10^3 = 1{\cdot}73 \times 3{\cdot}78 \times 10^7.$

Setting 1 on C to 1·73 on D, we read, under 3·78 on C, the result of the simple multiplication, as 6·54. Multiplying by 10^7 moves the decimal point 7 places to the right, and the answer is 65,400,000.

If it is required to find a series of products of which one of the factors is *constant*, set 1 on C to the constant factor on D and read the several products on D, under the respective variable factors.

If the factors are required which will give a constant *product* (really a case of division), set the cursor to the constant product on D. Then obviously, as the slide is moved along, any pair of factors found simultaneously under the cursor line on C, and on D under index of C, will give the product. A better method of working will be explained when we deal with the inversion of the slide.

It is sometimes useful to remember that although we usually set the slide to the rule, we can obtain the result equally well by setting the rule to the slide. Thus, bringing 1 (or 10) on D to 2 on C, we find on C, *over* any other factor, n on D, the product of $2 \times n$. But note that the slide and rule have now changed places, and if we use rules for the number of digits in the result, we must now deduct 1 from the sum of the digits in the factors, when the *rule projects* to the *right of the slide*.

With the ordinary 10in. rule it will be found in general that the extent to which the C and D scales are subdivided is such as to enable not more than three figures in either factor being dealt with. For the same reason it is impossible to directly read more than the first three figures of any product, although it is often possible—by mentally dividing the smallest space involved in the reading—to correctly determine the fourth figure of a product. Necessarily this method is only reliable when used in the earlier parts of the C and D scales. However, the last numeral of a three-figure, and in some cases the last of a four-figure, product can be readily ascertained by an inspection of the factors.

Ex.—19 × 27 = 513. Placing the L.H. index of C to 19 on D, we find opposite 27 on C, the product, which lies between 510 and 515. A glance at the factors, however, is sufficient to decide that the third figure must be 3, since the product of 9 and 7 is 63, and the last figure of this product must be the last figure in the answer.

Ex.—79 × 91 = 7189.

In this case the division line 91 on C indicates on D that the answer lies between 7180 and 7190. As the last figure must be 9, it is at once inferred that the last two figures are 89.

When there are more than three figures in either or both of the factors, the fourth and following figures to the right must be neglected. It is well to note, however, that if the first neglected figure is 5, or greater than 5, it will generally be advisable to increase by 1 the third figure of the factor employed. Generally it will suffice to make this increase in one of the two factors only, but it is obvious that in some cases greater accuracy will be obtained by increasing both factors in this way.

CONTINUED MULTIPLICATION.—To find the product of more than two factors, we make use of the cursor to mark the position of successive products (the value of which does not concern us) as the several factors are taken into the calculation. Setting the index of C to the 1st factor on D, we bring the line of the cursor to the 2nd factor on C, then the index of C to the cursor, the cursor to the 3rd factor, index of C to cursor, and so on, reading the final product on D under the last factor on C. (Note that the 1st factor and the result are read on D; all intermediate readings are taken on C.)

If the rule for the number of digits in a product is used, it is necessary to note the number of times multiplication is effected with the slide projecting to the right. This number, deducted from the sum of the digits of the several factors, gives the number of digits in the product. Ingenious devices have been adopted to record the number of times the slide projects to the right, but some of these are very inconvenient. The author's method is to record each time the slide so projects, by a minus mark, thus -. These can be noted down in any convenient manner, and the sum of the marks so obtained deducted from the sum of the digits in the several factors, gives the number of digits in the product as before explained.

Ex.—$42 \times 71 \times 1.5 \times 0.32 \times 121 = 173,200$.

The product given, which is that read on the rule, is obtained as follows:—Set R.H. index of C to 42 on D, and bring the cursor to 71 on C. Next bring the L.H. index of C to the cursor, and the latter to 1·5 on C. This multiplication is effected with the slide to the right, and a memorandum of this fact is kept by making a mark -. Bring the R.H. index of C to the cursor and the latter to 0·32 on C. Then set the L.H. index of C to the cursor and read the result, 1732, on D under 121 on C, while as a slide again projects to the right, a second-memo-mark is recorded. There are $2+2+1+0+3=8$ digits in the factors, and as there were 2-marks recorded during the operation, there will be $8-2=6$ digits in the product, which will therefore read 173,200 (173,194·56).

For a very rough evaluation of the result, we note that $1·5 \times 0·3$ is about 0·5; hence, as a clue to the number of figures we have
$$40 \times 70 \times 60 = 3000 \times 60 = 180,000.$$

DIVISION

The instructions for multiplication having been given in some detail, a full discussion of the inverse process of division will be unnecessary.

RULE FOR DIVISION.—*Place the divisor on C, opposite the dividend on D, and read the quotient on D under the index of C.*

Ex.—$225 \div 18 = 12·5$.

Bringing 18 on C to 225 on D, we find 12·5 under the L.H. index of C.

As in multiplication, the factors are treated as whole numbers, and the position of the decimal point afterwards decided according to the following rule, which, as will be seen, is the reverse of that for multiplication :—

RULE FOR THE NUMBER OF DIGITS IN A QUOTIENT.—*If the quotient is read with the slide projecting to the* LEFT, *subtract the number of digits in the divisor from those in the dividend; but if read with the slide to the* RIGHT, ADD 1 *to this difference.**

In the above example the quotient is read off with the slide to the right, so the number of digits in the answer $= 3 - 2 \times 1 = 2$.

Ex.—$0·000221 \div 0·017 = 0·013$.

Here the number of digits in the dividend is -3, and in the divisor -1. The difference is -2; but as the result is obtained with the slide to the right, this result must be increased by 1, so that the number of digits in the quotient is $-2 + 1 = -1$, giving the answer as 0·013.

If preferred, the result can be obtained in the manner referred to when considering the multiplication of decimals. Thus, treating the above as whole numbers, we find that the result of dividing 221 by $17 = 13$, since the difference in the number of digits in the factors, which is 1, is, owing to the position of the slide, increased by 1, giving 2 as the number of digits in the answer. Then by the

---

* The special case in which the numerator is 1, 10, or any power of 10 must be treated by the rule for reciprocals (page 27).

rules for the division of decimals we know that the number of decimal places in the quotient is equal to $6-3=3$, showing that a cypher is to be prefixed to the result read on the rule.

As in multiplication, so in division, we have a

GENERAL RULE FOR NUMBER OF DIGITS IN A QUOTIENT.—*When the first significant figure in the* DIVISOR *is greater than that in the* DIVIDEND, *the number of digits in the quotient is found by subtracting the digits in the divisor from those in the dividend. When the contrary is the case,* 1 IS TO BE ADDED *to this difference. When the first figures are the same, those following must be compared.*

ESTIMATION OF THE FIGURES IN A QUOTIENT.—The method of roughly estimating the number of figures in a quotient needs little explanation.

Ex.—$3·95 \div 5340 = 0·00074$.

Setting 534 on C to 3·95 on D we read under the (R.H.) index of C, the significant figures on D, which are 74. Then $3·9 \div 5$ is about 0·8 and $0·8 \div 1000$ gives 0·0008 as a rough estimate.

Ex.—$0·00000285 \div 0·000197 = 0·01446$.

Regarding this as $2·85 \times 10^{-6} \div 1·97 \times 10^{-4}$ we divide 2·85 by 1·97 and obtain 1·446. Dividing the powers of 10 we have $10^{-6} \div 10^{-4} = 10^{-2}$, so the decimal point is to be moved two places to the left and the answer is read as 0·01446.

Another method of dividing deserves mention as of special service when dividing a number of quantities by a *constant divisor*:—Set the index of C to the divisor on D and over any dividend on D, read the quotient on C.

For the division of a *constant dividend* by a variable divisor, set the cursor to the dividend on D and bring the divisor on C successively to the cursor, reading the corresponding quotients on D under the index of C. Another method which avoids moving the slide is explained in the section on "Multiplication and Division with the Slide Inverted."

CONTINUED DIVISION, if we can so call such an expression as

$$\frac{3·14}{785 \times 0·00021 \times 4·3 \times 64·4} = 0·0688,$$

may be worked by repeating as follows:—Set 7·85 on C to 3·14 on D, bring cursor to index of C, 2·1 on C to cursor, cursor to index, 4·3 to cursor, cursor to index, 6·44 to cursor, and under index of C read 688 on D as the significant figures of the answer.

For the number of figures in the result, we deduct the sum of the number of digits in the several factors and add 1 for each time the slide projects to the right, which in this case occurs once. There are $3+(-3)+1+2=3$ denominator digits, 1 numerator digit, and 1 is to be added to the difference. Therefore there are $1-3+1=-1$ digits in the answer, which is therefore 0·0688. The foregoing method of working may confuse the beginner, who is apt to fall into the process of continued multiplication. For this reason, until familiarity with combined methods has been acquired, the product of the several denominators should be first found by the continued multiplication process, and the figures in this product determined. Then divide the numerator by this product to obtain the result.

As the denominator product will be read on D, we may avoid resetting the slide by bringing the numerator on C to this product and reading the result on C *over* the index of D. The slide and rule have here changed places; hence if rules are followed for the number of figures in the result, 1 must be added to the difference of digits, when the *rule projects* to the *right of the slide*.

The author's method of recording the number of times division is performed with the slide to the right is by vertical memorandum marks, thus |. The full significance of these memo-marks will appear in the following section.

For a rough calculation to fix the decimal point, in this example we move the decimal points in the factors, obtaining

$$\frac{3}{0·8 \times 2 \times 4 \times 6} = \frac{3}{40} = 0·075.$$

THE USE OF THE UPPER SCALES FOR MULTIPLICATION AND DIVISION.

MANY prefer to use the upper scales A and B, in preference to C and D. The disadvantage is that as the scales are only one-half the length of C or D, the graduation does not permit of the same degree of accuracy being obtained as when working with the lower scales. But the result can always be read directly from the rule without ever having to change the position of the slide after it has been initially set. Hence, it obviates the uncertainty as to the direction in which the slide is to be moved in making a setting.

When the A and B scales are employed, it is understood that the left-hand pair of scales are to be used in the same manner as C and D, and so far the rules relating to the latter are entirely applicable. But in this case the slide is always moved to the right, so that in multiplication the product is found either upon the left or right scales of A. If it is found on the left A scale, the rule for the number of digits in the product is found as for the C and D scales, and is equal to the *sum of the digits in the two factors, minus* 1; but if found on the right-hand A scale, the number of digits in the product is equal to the sum of the digits in the two factors.

In division, similar modifications are necessary. If when moving the slide to the right the division can be completely effected by using the L.H. scale of A, the quotient (read on A above the L.H. of index B) has a number of digits equal to the number in the dividend, less the number in the divisor, *plus* 1. But if the division necessitates the use of both the A scales, the number of digits in the quotient equals the number in the dividend, less the number in the divisor.

RECIPROCALS.

A SPECIAL case of division, to be considered is the determination of the *reciprocal* of a number n, or $\frac{1}{n}$. Following the ordinary rule for division, it is evident that setting n on C to 1 on D, gives $\frac{1}{n}$ on D under 1 on C. It is more important to observe that by inverting the operation—setting 1 (or 10) on C to n on D—we can read $\frac{1}{n}$ on C over 1 (or 10) on D. Hence whenever a result is read on D under an index of C, we can also read its reciprocal on C over whichever index of D is available.

The Number of Digits in a Reciprocal is obvious when $n=10$, 100, or any power (p) of 10. Thus $\frac{1}{10}=0\cdot 1$; $\frac{1}{100}=0\cdot 01$; $\frac{1}{10^p}=1$ preceded by $p-1$ cyphers. For all other cases we have the rule:— *Subtract from* 1 *the number of digits in the number.*

Ex.—$\frac{1}{339}=0\cdot 00295$.

There are 3 digits in the number; hence, there are $1-3=-2$ digits in the answer.

Ex.—$\frac{1}{0\cdot 0000156}=64,100$.

There are -4 digits in the number; hence, there are $1-(-4)=5$ digits in the result.

CONTINUED MULTIPLICATION AND DIVISION.

By combining the rules for multiplication and division, we can readily evaluate expressions of the form $\frac{a}{b} \times \frac{c}{d} \times \frac{e}{f} \times \frac{g}{h} = x$. The simplest case, $\frac{a \times c}{b}$ can be solved by one setting of the slide.*

Take as an example, $\frac{14\cdot45 \times 60}{8\cdot5} = 102$. Setting 8·5 on C to 14·45 on D, we can, if desired, read 1·7 on D under 1 on C, as the quotient. However, we are not concerned with this, but require its multiplication by 60, and the slide being already set for this operation, we at once read under 60 on C the result, 102, on D. The figures in the answer are obvious.

When there are more factors to take into account, we place the cursor over 102 on D, bring the next divisor on C to the cursor, move the cursor to the next multiplier on C, bring the next divisor on C to the cursor, and so on, until all the factors have been dealt with. Note that only the first factor and the result are read on D; also *that the cursor is moved for multiplying and the slide for dividing.*

Number of Digits in Result in Combined Multiplication and Division.—For those who use rules the author's method of determining the decimal point in combined multiplication and division may be used. Each time *multiplication* is performed with the slide projecting to the *right*, make a − mark; each time *division* is effected with the slide to the right, make a | mark; *but allow the | marks to cancel the − marks as far as they will.* Subtract the sum of the digits in the denominator from the sum of digits in the numerator, and to this difference *add* any uncancelled memo-marks, if of | character, or *subtract* them if of − character.

Ex.— $\frac{43\cdot5 \times 29\cdot4 \times 51 \times 32}{27 \times 3\cdot83 \times 10\cdot5 \times 1\cdot31} = 1468$.

Set 27 on C to 43·5 on D, and as with this *division* the slide is to the right, make the first | mark. Bring cursor to 29·4 on C, and as in this *multiplication* the slide is to the right, make the first − mark, cancelling as shown.

---

* The possible need for traversing the slide, to change the indices, when using the C and D scales, is not considered as a setting.

Setting 3·83 on C to the cursor, requires the second ∣ mark, which, however, is cancelled in turn by the multiplication by 51. The division by 10·5 requires the third ∣ mark, and after multiplying by 32 (requiring no mark) the final division by 1·31 requires the fourth ∣ mark. Then, as there are 8 numerator digits, 6 denominator, and 2 uncancelled memo-marks (which, being ∣, are additive) we have

$$\text{Number of digits in result} = 8 - 6 + 2 = 4.$$

Had the uncancelled marks been − in character, the number of digits would have been $8 - 6 - 2 = 0$.

For quantities less than 0·1 the digit place numbers will be *negative*. The troublesome addition of these may be avoided by transferring them to the opposite side and treating them as positive. Thus:—

$$\frac{\overset{2}{0\cdot00356} \times 27\cdot1 \times \overset{4}{0\cdot08375}}{\underset{2}{0\cdot1426} \times \underset{1}{9\cdot85} \times \underset{1}{0\cdot00002}} = 288.$$

The first numerator, 0·00356, has −2 digits. Note this by placing 2 *below the lower line* as shown. 27·1 has 2 digits; place 2 over it. 0·08375 has −1 digit; hence place 1 *below the lower line*. The first denominator has no digits; the second, 9·85, has 1 digit; hence place 1 under it. 0·00002 has −4 digits; place 4 *above the upper line*. The sum of the top series is $2+4=6$; of the bottom series $2+1+1=4$. Subtracting the bottom from the top, we have $6-4=2$ digits, to which 1 has to be added for an uncancelled memo-mark, and the result is read as 288.

Moving the decimal point often facilitates matters. Thus, $\dfrac{32\cdot4 \times 0\cdot98 \times 432 \times 0\cdot0217}{4\cdot71 \times 0\cdot175 \times 0\cdot00000621 \times 412000}$ is much more conveniently dealt with when re-arranged as $\dfrac{32\cdot4 \times 9\cdot8 \times 432 \times 2\cdot17}{4\cdot71 \times 17\cdot5 \times 6\cdot21 \times 4\cdot12} = 141.$

To determine the number of figures in the result by rough cancelling and mental calculation, we note that 4·71 enters 432 about 100 times; 9·8 enters 17·5 about 2, 6·21 into 32·4 about 5; and 2·17 into 4·12 about 2. This gives $\dfrac{500}{4} = 125$, showing that the result contains 3 digits. From the slide rule we read 141, which is therefore the result sought.

The occasional traversing of the slide through the rule, to interchange the indices—a contingency which the use of the C and D scales always involves—may often be avoided by a very simple expedient. Such an example as $\frac{6\cdot19 \times 31\cdot2 \times 422}{1120 \times 8\cdot86 \times 2\cdot09} = 3\cdot93$ is sometimes cited as a particularly difficult case. Working through the expression as given, two traversings of the slide are necessary; but by taking the factors in the slightly different order, $\frac{6\cdot19 \times 31\cdot2 \times 422}{8\cdot86 \times 2\cdot09 \times 1120}$, *so that the significant figures of each pair are more nearly alike*, we not only avoid any traversing the slide, but we also reduce the extent to which the slide is moved to effect the several divisions.

Such cases as $\frac{a \times b}{c \times d \times e \times f \times g}$ or $\frac{a \times b \times c \times d \times e}{f \times g}$ really resolve themselves into $\frac{a \times b \times 1 \times 1 \times 1}{c \times d \times e \times f \times g}$ and $\frac{a \times b \times c \times d \times e}{f \times g \times 1 \times 1 \times 1}$, but, of course, if rules are used to locate the decimal point, the 1's so (mentally) introduced are not to be counted as additional figures in the factors.

MULTIPLICATION AND DIVISION WITH THE SLIDE INVERTED.

If the slide be inverted in the rule but with the same face uppermost, so that the C scale lies adjacent to the A scale, and the right and left indices of the slide and rule are placed in coincidence, we find the product of any number on D by the coincident number on C (readily referred to each other by the cursor) is always 10. Hence, by reading the numbers on C as decimals, we have over any unit number on D, its *reciprocal* on C. Thus 2 on D is found opposite 0·5 on C; 3 on D opposite to 0·333; while opposite 8 on C is 0·125 on D, etc. The reason of this is that the sum of the lengths of the slide and rule corresponding to the factors, is always equal to the length corresponding to the product—in this case, 10.

It will be seen that if we attempt to apply the ordinary rule for multiplication, with the slide inverted, we shall actually be multiplying the one factor taken on D by the *reciprocal* of the other taken on C. But multiplying by the *reciprocal of a number* is equivalent to *dividing* by that number, and *dividing* a factor by the *reciprocal* of a number is equivalent to *multiplying* by that number. It follows that with the slide inverted the operations of multiplication and division are reversed, as are also the rules for the number of digits in the product and the position of the decimal point. Hence, in multiplying with the slide inverted, we place (by the aid of the cursor) one factor on C opposite the other factor on D, and read the result on D under either index of C. It follows that with the slide thus set, any pair of coinciding factors on C and D will give the same constant product found on D under the index of C. One useful application of this fact is found in selecting the scantlings of rectangular sections of given areas or in deciding upon the dimensions of rectangular sheets, plates, cisterns, etc. Thus by placing the index of C to 72 on D, it is readily seen that a plate having an area of 72 sq. ft. may have sides 8 by 9 ft., 6 by 12, 5 by 14·4, 4 by 18, 3 by 24, 2 by 36, with innumerable intermediate values. Many other useful applications of a similar character will suggest themselves.

PROPORTION.

WITH the slide in the ordinary position and with the indices of the C and D scales in exact agreement, the *ratio* of the corresponding divisions of these scales is 1. If the slide is moved so that 1 on C agrees with 2 on D, we know that under any number n on C is $n \times 2$ on D, so that if we read numerators on C and denominators on D we have

C	1	1·5	2	3	4
D1	2	3	4	6	8

In other words, the numbers on D bear to the coinciding numbers on C a ratio of 2 to 1. Obviously the same condition will obtain no matter in what position the slide may be placed. The rule for proportion, which is apparent from the foregoing, may be expressed as follows :—

RULE FOR PROPORTION.—*Set the first term of a proportion on the C scale to the second term on the D scale, and opposite the third term on the C scale read the fourth term on the D scale.*

Ex.—Find the 4th term in the proportion of 20 : 27 : : 70 : x.

Set 20 on C to 27 on D, and opposite 70 on C read 94·5 on D.

Thus
C	20	70
D	27	94·5

It will be evident that this is merely a case of combined multiplication and division of the form, $\frac{20 \times 70}{27} = 94\cdot5$. Hence, given any three terms of a proportion, we set the 1st to the 2nd, or the 3rd to the 4th, as the case may be, and opposite the other given term read the term required.*

Thus, in reducing vulgar fractions to decimals, the decimal equivalent of $\frac{3}{16}$ is determined by placing 3 on C to 16 on D, when over the index or 1 of D we read 0·1875 on C. In this case the terms are $3 : 16 :: x : 1$. For the inverse operation—to find a vulgar fraction equivalent to a given decimal—the given decimal fraction on C is set to the index of D, and then opposite any denominator on D is the corresponding numerator of the fraction on C.

If the index of C be placed to agree with 3·1416 on D, it will be clear from what has been said that this ratio exists throughout between the numbers of the two scales. Therefore, against any *diameter* of a circle on C will be found the corresponding *circumference* on D. In the same way, by setting 1 on C to the appropriate conversion factor on D, we can convert a series of values in one denomination to their equivalents in another denomination. In this connection the following table of conversion factors will be found of service. If the A and B scales are used instead of the C and D scales, a complete set of conversions will be at once obtained. In this case, however, the left-hand A and B scales should be used for the initial setting, any values read on the right-hand A or B scales being read as of tenfold value. With the C and D scales a portion of the one scale will project beyond the other. To read this portion of the scale, the cursor or runner is brought to whichever index of the C scale falls within the rule, and the slide moved until the other index of the C scale coincides with the cursor, when the remainder of the equivalent values can then be read off. It must be remembered that if the slide is moved in the direction of notation (to the *right*), the values read thereon have a tenfold *greater* value; if the slide is moved to the *left*, the readings thereon are *decreased* in a tenfold degree. Although preferred by many, in the form given, the case is obviously one of multiplication, and is so treated in the Data Slips at the end of the book.

---

* The reader may be reminded that cross-multiplication of the factors in any such slide rule setting will give a constant product, *e.g.*, $20 \times 94·5 = 27 \times 70$.

TABLE OF CONVERSION FACTORS.

GEOMETRICAL EQUIVALENTS.

SCALE C.	SCALE D.	If C=1, D=
Diameter of circle	Circumference of circle	3·1416
,, ,,	Side of inscribed square	0·707
,, ,,	,, equal square	0·886
,, ,,	,, equilateral triangle	1·346
Circum. of circle	,, inscribed square	0·225
,, ,,	,, equal square	0·282
Side of square	Diagonal of square	1·414
Square inch	Circular inch	1·273
Area of circle	Area of inscribed square	0·636

MEASURES OF AREA.

SCALE C.	SCALE D.	If C=1, D=
Square inches	Square centimetres	6·45
Circular ,,	,, ,,	5·067
Square feet	,, metres	0·0929
,, yards	,, ,,	0·836
,, miles	,, kilometres	2·59
Acres	Hectares	259·00
,,	,,	0·4046

MEASURES OF LENGTH.

		If C=1, D=
Inches	Millimetres	25·40
,,	Centimetres	2·54
8ths of an inch	Millimetres	3·175
16ths ,, ,,	,,	1·587
32nds ,, ,,	,,	0·794
64ths ,, ,,	,,	0·397
Feet	Metres	0·3048
Yards	,,	0·9144
Chains	,,	20·116
Miles	Kilometres	1·609

MEASURES OF CAPACITY.

		If C=1, D=
Cubic inches	Cubic centimetres	16·38
,, ,,	Imperial gallons	0·00360
,, ,,	U.S. gallons	0·00432
,, ,,	Litres	0·01638
Cubic feet	Cubic metres	0·0283
,, ,,	Imperial gallons	6·23
,, ,,	U.S. gallons	7·48
,, ,,	Litres	28·37
,, yards	Cubic metres	0·764
Imperial gallons	Litres	4·54
,, ,,	U.S. gallons	1·200
Bushels	Cubic metres	0·0363
,,	,, feet	1·283

TABLE OF CONVERSION FACTORS—Continued.

Measures of Weight.

Scale C.	Scale D.	If C=1, D=
Grains	Grammes	0·0648
Ounces (Troy)	,,	31·103
,, (Avoird.)	,,	28·35
,, ,,	Kilogrammes	0·02835
Pounds (Troy)	,,	0·3732
,, (Avoird.)	,,	0·4536
Hundredweights	,,	50·802
Tons	,,	1016·04
,,	Metric tonnes	1·016

Compound Factors—Velocities.

Scale C.	Scale D.	If C=1, D=
Feet per second	Metres per second	0·3048
,, ,,	,, minute	18·288
,, ,, minute	Miles per hour	·682
,, ,,	Metres per second	0·00508
,, ,,	,, minute	0·3048
,, ,,	Miles per hour	0·01136
Yards per ,,	,, ,,	0·0341
Miles per hour	Metres per minute	26·82
Knots	,, ,,	30·88
,,	Miles per hour	1·151

Compound Factors—Pressures.

Scale C.	Scale D.	If C=1, D=
Pounds per sq. inch	Grammes per sq. mm.	0·7031
,, ,, ,,	Kilos. per sq. centimetre	0·0703
,, ,, ,,	Atmospheres	0·068
,, ,, ,,	Head of water in inches	27·71
,, ,, ,,	,, ,, feet	2·309
,, ,, ,,	,, ,, metres	0·757
Inches of water	Inches of Mercury	2·04
,, ,,	Pounds per square inch	0·0361
,, ,,	Inches of mercury	0·0714
Inches of mercury	Pounds per square foot	5·20
Atmospheres	,, ,,	0·0333
,,	Metres of water	10·34
Feet of water	Kilos. per sq. cm.	1·033
,, ,,	Pounds per square foot	62·35
,, ,,	Atmospheres	0·0294
,, ,,	Inches of mercury	0·883
Pounds per sq. foot	,, ,,	0·01417
,, ,,	Kilos. per square metre	4·883
,, ,,	Atmospheres	0·000472
Pounds per sq. yard	Kilos. per square metre	0·5425
Tons per sq. inch	,, square mm.	1·575
,, sq. foot	Tonnes per square metre	10·93b

TABLE OF CONVERSION FACTORS—Continued.

COMPOUND FACTORS—WEIGHTS, CAPACITIES, ETC.

SCALE C.	SCALE D.	If C=1, D=
Pounds per lineal ft.	Kilos. per lineal metre	1·488
,, per lineal yd.	,, ,, ,,	0·496
,, per lineal mile	Kilos. per kilometre	0·2818
Tons ,, ,,	Tonnes ,, ,,	0·6313
Feet ,, ,,	Metres ,, ,,	1·894
Pounds per cubic in.	Grammes per cubic cm.	27·68
,, per cubic ft.	Kilos. per cubic metre	16·02
,, per cubic yd.	,, ,, ,,	0·593
Tons per cubic yard.	Tonnes ,, ,,	1·329
Cubic yds. per pound	Cubic metres per kilo.	1·685
,, ,, per ton..	,, ,, per tonne..	0·7525
Cubic inch of water.	Weight in pounds	0·03608
Cubic feet of water..	,, ,, kilos	28·23
,, ,, ,,	Imperial gallons	6·235
,, ,, ,,	U.S. gallons	7·48
Litre of water	Cubic inches	61·025
Gallons of water....	Weight in kilos.	4·54
Pounds of fresh water	Pounds of sea water	1·026
Grains per gallon....	Grammes per litre	0·01426
Pounds per gallon..	Kilos. per litre	0·0998
,, per U.S. gal.	,, ,,	0·115

COMPOUND FACTORS—POWER UNITS, ETC.

SCALE C.	SCALE D.	If C=1, D=
British Ther. Units.	Kilogrammetres	108
,, ,,	Joules	1058
,, ,,	Calories (Fr. Ther. units)	0·252
,, per sq. ft.	,, per square metre	2·713
,, per pound	,, per kilogramme	0·555
Pounds per sq. ft.	Dynes, per sq. cm.	479
Foot-pounds	Kilogrammetres	0·1382
,, ,,	Joules	1·356
,, ,,	Calorie	0·00129
Foot-tons	Tonne-metres	0·000324
Horse-power	Force de cheval (Fr.H.P.)	0·333
,, ,,	Kilowatts	1·014
Pounds per H.P.	Kilos. per cheval	0·746
Square feet per H.P.	Square metres per cheval	0·447
Cubic ,, ,,	Cubic ,, ,,	0·0196
Watts	,,	0·0279
,,	Ther. Units per hour	3·44
,,	Foot-pounds per second	0·73
,,	,, per minute.	44·24
Watt-hours	Kilogrammetres	367
,, ,,	Joules	3600
Kilogrammetres	,,	9·806

Inverse Proportion.—If "more" requires "less," or "less" requires "more," the case is one of *inverse* proportion, and although it will be seen that this form of proportion is quite readily dealt with by the preceding method, the working is simplified to some extent by inverting the slide so that the C scale is adjacent to the A scale. By the aid of the cursor, the values on the inverted C (or O) scale, and on the D scale, can be then read off. These will now constitute a series of inverse ratios. For example, in the proportion

O	8	4
D	1·5	3

the 4 on the O scale is brought opposite 3 on D, when under 8 on O is found 1·5 on D.*

GENERAL HINTS ON THE ELEMENTARY USES OF THE SLIDE RULE.

BEFORE the more complex operations of involution, evolution, etc., are considered, a few general hints on the use of the slide rule for elementary operations may be of service, especially as these will serve to enforce some of the more important points brought out in the preceding sections.

Always use the slide rule in as *direct* a light as possible.

Study the manner in which the scales are divided. Follow the graduations of the C and D scales from 1 to 10, noting the values given by each successive graduation and how these values change as we follow along to the right. Do the same with the two halves of the A and B scales and note the difference in the value of the subdivisions, due to the shorter scale-lengths.

Practise reading values by setting 1 on C to some value on D and reading under 2, 3, 4, etc., on C, checking the readings by mental arithmetic. To the same end, find squares, square roots, etc., comparing the results with the actual values as given in tables. Practise setting both slide and cursor to values taken at random. Aim at accuracy; speed will come with practice.

---

* In this case cross-*dividing* gives a constant quotient, *e.g.*, $8 \div 3 = 4 \div 1·5$. Since the upper scale is now a scale of reciprocals, the ratio is really

O	$\frac{1}{8}$	$\frac{1}{4}$
D	1·5	3
.

When in doubt as to any method of working, verify by making a simple calculation of the same form.

Follow the orthodox methods of working until entirely confident in the use of the instrument, and even then do not readily make a change. If any altered procedure is adopted, first work a simple case and guard carefully against unconsciously lapsing into the usual method during the operation.

Unless the calculation is of a straightforward character, time taken in considering how best to attack it (rearranging the expression if desirable) is generally time well spent.

In setting two values together, set the cursor to one of them on the rule, and bring the other, on the slide, to the cursor line.

In multiplying factors, as 57×0.1256, take the fractional value first. It is easier to set 1 on C to 1256 on D and read under 57 on C, than to reverse the procedure. When both values are eye-estimated, set the cursor to the second factor on C and read the result on D, under the cursor line.

In continuous operations avoid moving the slide further than necessary, by taking the factors in that order which will keep the scale readings as close together as possible.

SQUARES AND SQUARE ROOTS.

WE have seen that the relation which the upper scales bear to the lower set is such that over any number on D is its *square* on A, and, conversely, under any number on A is its *square root* on D, the same remarks applying to the C and B scales on the slide. Taking the values engraved on the rule, we have on D, numbers lying between 1 and 10, and on A the corresponding squares extending from 1 to 100. Hence the squares of numbers between 1 and 10, or the roots of numbers between 1 and 100, can be read off on the rule by the aid of the cursor. All other cases are brought within these ranges of values by factorising with powers of 10, as before explained.

The more practical rule is the following :—

To Find the Square of a Number, set the cursor to the number on D and read the required square on A under the cursor. The rule for

The Number of Digits in a Square is easily deducible from the rule for multiplication. If the square is read on the *left* scale of **A, it**

will contain *twice* the number of digits in the original number *less* 1; if it is read on the *right* scale of A, it will contain *twice* the number of digits in the original number.

Ex.—Find the square of 114.

Placing the cursor to 114 on D, it is seen that the coinciding number on A is 13. As the result is read off on the *left* scale of A, the number of digits will be $(3 \times 2) - 1 = 5$, and the answer is read as 13,000. The true result is 12,996.

Ex.—Find the square of 0·0093.

The cursor being placed to 93 on D, the number on A is found to be 865. The result is read on the *right* scale of A, so the number of digits $= -2 \times 2 = -4$, and the answer is read as 0·0000865 [0·00008649].

Square Root.—The foregoing rules suggest the method of procedure in the inverse operation of extracting the square root of a given number, which will be found on the D scale opposite the number on the A scale. It is necessary to observe, however, that if the number consists of an *odd* number of digits, it is to be taken on the *left-hand* portion of the A scale, and the number of digits in the root $= \dfrac{N+1}{2}$, N being the number of digits in the original number. When there is an *even* number of digits in the number, it is to be taken on the *right-hand* portion of the A scale, and the root contains *one-half* the number of digits in the original number.

Ex.—Find the square root of 36,500.

As there is an *odd* number of digits, placing the cursor to 365 on the L.H. A scale gives 191 on D. By the rule there are $\dfrac{N+1}{2} = \dfrac{5+1}{2} = 3$ digits in the required root, which is therefore read as 191 [191·05].

Ex.—Find $\sqrt{0·0098}$.

Placing the cursor to 98 on the right-hand scale of A (since -2 is an *even* number of digits), it is seen that the coinciding number on D is 99. As the number of digits in the number is -2, the number of digits in the root will be $\dfrac{-2}{2} = -1$. It will therefore be read as 0·099 [0·09899+].

Ex.—Find $\sqrt{0·098}$.

The number of digits is -1, so under 98 on the left scale of A, we find 313 on D. By the rule the number in the root will be $\frac{-1+1}{2}=0$, and the root is therefore read as 0·313 [0·313049+].

Ex.—Find $\sqrt{0\cdot 149}$.

As the number of digits (0) is *even*, the cursor is set to 149 on the right-hand scale of A, giving 386 on D. By the rule, the number of digits in the root will be $\frac{0}{2}=0$, and the root will be read as 0·386 [0·38605+].

Another method of extracting the square root, by which more accurate readings may generally be obtained, is by using the C and D scales only, with the slide inverted. If there is an *odd* number of digits in the number, the *right* index, or if an *even* number of digits the *left* index, of the inverted scale O is placed so as to coincide with the number on D of which the root is sought. Then with the cursor, the number is found on D which coincides with the same number on O, which number is the root sought.

Ex.—Find $\sqrt{22\cdot 2}$.

Placing the left index of O to 222 on D, the two equal coinciding numbers on O and D are found to be 4·71.

Note that under the cursor line we have the original number, 22·2, on A, and from this the number of digits in the root is determined as before.

The plan of finding the square of a number by ordinary multiplication is often very convenient. The inverse process of finding a square root by trial division is not to be recommended.

To obtain a close value of a root or to verify one found in the usual way, the author has, on occasion, adopted the following plan:—Set 1 (or 10) on B to the number on the A scale (L.H. or R.H as the case may require), and bring the cursor to the number on D. If the root found is correct, the readings on C under the cursor and on D under the index of C, will be in exact agreement.

If 1 on B is placed to a number n on the L.H. A scale, the student will note that while root n is read on D under 1 on C, the root of 10 n is read on D under 10 on B. Hence, if preferred, the number can be taken always on the first scale of A and the root read under 1 or 10 on B, according to whether there is an odd or even number of digits in the number. Obviously the second root is the first multiplied by $\sqrt{10}$.

CUBES AND CUBE ROOTS.

In raising a number to the third power, a combination of the preceding method and ordinary multiplication is employed.

To Find the Cube of a Number.—*Set the* L.H. *or* R.H. *index of C to the number on D, and opposite the number* on the left-hand *scale of B read the cube on the* L.H. *or* R.H. *scale of A.*

By this rule four scales are brought into requisition. Of these, the D scale and the L.H. B scale are *always* employed, and are to be read as of equal denomination. The values assigned to the L.H. and R.H. scales of A will be apparent from the following considerations.

Commencing with the indices of C and D coinciding, and moving the slide to the right, it will be seen that, working in accordance with the above rule, the cubes of numbers from 1 to 2·154 ($=\sqrt[3]{10}$) will be found on the first or L.H. scale of A. Moving the slide still farther to the right, we obtain *on the* R.H. *A scale* cubes of numbers from 2·154 to 4·641 (or $\sqrt[3]{10}$ to $\sqrt[3]{100}$). Had we a *third* repetition of the L.H. A scale, the L.H. index of C could be still further traversed to the right, and the cubes of numbers from 4·641 to 10 read off on this prolongation of A. But the same end can be attained by making use of the R.H. index of C, when, traversing the slide to the right as before, the cubes of numbers from 4·641 to 10 on D can be read off *on the* L.H. *A scale* over the corresponding numbers on the L.H. B scale. Hence, using the L.H. index of C, the readings on the L.H. A scale may be regarded comparatively as units, those on the R.H. A scale as tens; while for the hundreds we again make use of the L.H. A scale in conjunction with the *right-hand* index of C.

By keeping these points in view, the number of digits in the cube (N) of a given number (n) are readily deduced. Thus, if the units scale is used, $N = 3n - 2$; if the tens scale, $N = 3n - 1$; while if the hundreds scale be used, $N = 3n$. Placed in the form of rules:—

$N = 3n - 2$ when the product is read on the L.H. scale of A with the slide to the *right* (units scale).

$N = 3n - 1$ when the product is read on the R.H. scale of A; slide to the *right* (tens scale).

$N = 3n$ when the product is read on the L.H. scale of A with the slide to the *left* (hundreds scale).

With decimals the same rule applies, but, as before, the number of digits must be read as -1, -2, etc., when one, two, etc., cyphers follow immediately after the decimal point.

Ex.—Find the value of $1{\cdot}4^3$.

Placing the L.H. index of C to 1·4 on D, the reading on A opposite 1·4 on the L.H. scale of B is found to be about 2·745 [2·744].

Ex.—Find the value of $26{\cdot}4^3$.

Placing the L.H. index of C to 26·4 on D, the reading on A opposite 26·4 on the L.H. scale of B is found to be about 18,400 [18,399·744].

Ex.—Find the value of $7{\cdot}3^3$.

In this case it becomes necessary to use the R.H. index of C, which is set to 7·3 on D, when opposite 7·3 on the L.H. scale of B is read 389 [389·017] on A.

Ex.—Find the value of $0{\cdot}073^3$.

From the setting as before it is seen that the number of digits in the number must be multiplied by 3. Hence, as there is -1 digit in 0·073, there will be -3 in the cube, which is therefore read 0·000389.

The last two examples serve to illustrate the principle of factorising with powers of 10. Thus

$$0{\cdot}073 = 7{\cdot}3 \times 10^{-2}; \quad 0{\cdot}073^3 = 7{\cdot}3^3 \times (10^{-2})^3 = 389 \times 10^{-6} = 0{\cdot}000389.$$

Cube Root (Direct Method).—One method of extracting the cube root of a number is by an inversion of the foregoing operation. Using the same scales, *the slide is moved either to the right or left until under the given number on A is found a number on the L.H. B scale, identical with the number simultaneously found on D under the right or left index of C.* This number is the required cube root.

From what has already been said regarding the combined use of these scales in cubing, it will be evident that in extracting the cube root of a number, it is necessary, in order to decide which scales are to be used, to know the number of figures to be dealt with. We therefore (as in the arithmetical method of extraction) point off the given number into sections of three figures each, commencing at the decimal point, and proceeding to the left for numbers greater than unity, and to the right for numbers less than unity. Then if the first section of figures on the left consists of—

1 figure, the number will evidently require to be taken on what we have called the "units" scale—*i.e.*, on the L.H. scale of A, using the L.H index of C.

If of 2 figures, the number will be taken on the "tens" scale—*i.e.*, on the R H. scale of A, using the L.H. index of C.

If of 3 figures, the number will be taken on the "hundreds" scale—*i.e.*, on the L.H. scale of A, using the R.H. index of C.

To determine the number of digits in cube roots it is only necessary to note that when the number is pointed off into sections as directed, there will be one figure in the root for every section into which the number is so divided, whether the *first* section consists of 1, 2, or 3 digits.

Of numbers wholly decimal, the cube roots will be decimal, and for every group of *three* 0s immediately following the decimal point, *one* 0 will follow the decimal point in the root. If necessary, 0s must be added so as to make up complete multiples of 3 figures before proceeding to extract the root. Thus 0·8 is to be regarded as 0·800, and 0·00008 as 0 000080 in extracting cube roots.

Ex.—Find $\sqrt[3]{14,000}$.

Pointing the number off in the manner described, it is seen that there are *two* figures in the first section—viz., 14. Setting the cursor to 14 on the R.H. scale of A, the slide is moved to the right until it is seen that 241 on the L.H. scale of B falls under the cursor, when 241 on D is under the L.H. index of C. Pointing 14,000 off into sections we have 14 000—that is, *two* sections. Therefore, there are two digits in the root, which in consequence will be read 24·1 [24·1014+].

Ex.—Find $\sqrt[3]{0·162}$.

As the divisional section consists of *three* figures, we use the "hundreds" scale. Setting the cursor to 0·162 on the L.H. A scale, and using the R.H. index of C, we move the slide to the left until under the cursor 0·545 is found on the L.H. B scale, while the R.H. index of C points to 0·545 on D, which is therefore the cube root of 0·162.

Ex.—Find $\sqrt[3]{0·0002}$.

To make even multiples of 3 figures requires the addition of 00; we have then 200, the cube root of which is found to be about 5·85. Then, since the first divisional group consists of 0s, one 0 will follow the decimal point, giving $\sqrt[3]{0·0002}$ = 0·0585 [0·05848].

Cube Root (Inverted Slide Method).—Another method of extracting the cube root involves the use of the inverted slide. Several methods are used, but the following is to be preferred :—*Set the* L.H. *or* R.H. *index of the slide to the number on A, and the number on Ƀ (i.e., B inverted), which coincides with the same number on D, is the required root.*

Setting the slide as directed, and using first the L.H. index of the slide and then the R.H. index, it is always possible to find *three* pairs of coincident values. To determine which of the three is the required result is best shown by an example.

Ex.—Find $\sqrt[3]{5}$, $\sqrt[3]{50}$, and $\sqrt[3]{500}$.

Setting the R.H. index of the slide to 5 on A, it is seen that 1·71 on D coincides with 1·71 on Ƀ. Then setting the L.H. index to 5 on A, further coincidences are found at 3·68 and at 7·93, the three values thus found being the required roots. Note that the first root was found on that portion of the D scale lying under 1 to 5 on A; the second root on that portion lying under 5 to 50 on A; and the third root on that portion of D lying under 50 to 100 on A. In this connection, therefore, scale A may always be considered to be divided into three sections—viz, 1 to n, n to 10 n, and 10 n to 100. For all numbers consisting of 1, 1+3, 1+6, 1+9 —*i.e.*, of 1, 4, 7, 10, or −2, −5, etc., figures—the coincidence under the first section is the one required. If the number has 2, 5, 8, or −1, −4, −7, etc., figures, the coincidence under the second section is correct, while if the number has 3, 6, 9, or 0, −3, etc., figures, the coincidence under the last section is that required. The number of digits in the root is determined by marking off the number into sections, as already explained.

Cube Root (Pickworth's Method).—One of the principal objections to the two methods described is the difficulty of recollecting which scales are to be employed and with which index of the slide they are to be used. With the direct method another objection is that the readings to be compared are often some distance apart, the maximum distance intervening being *two-thirds* of the length of the rule. To carry the eye from one to another is troublesome and time-taking. With the inverted scale method the reading of a scale reversed in direction and with the figures inverted is also objectionable.

With the author's method these objections are entirely obviated. The *same scales and index are always used*, and are read in their normal position. The three roots of n, $10n$ and $100n$ (n being less than 10 and not less than 1) are given with one setting and appear in their natural sequence, no traversing of the slide being needed. The readings to be compared are always close together, the maximum distance between them being *one-sixth* of the length of the rule. The setting is always made in the earlier part of the scales where closer readings can be obtained, and finally, if desired, the result may be readily verified on the lower scales by successive multiplication.

For this method two gauge points are required on C. To conveniently locate these, set 53 on C to 246 on D; join 1 on D to 1 on A with a straight-edge and with a needle point draw a short fine line on C. Set 246 on C to 53 on D, and repeat the process at the other end of the rule. The gauge points thus obtained (dividing C into three equal parts) will be at 2·154 and 4·641, and should be marked $\sqrt[3]{10}$ and $\sqrt[3]{100}$ respectively.*

Ex.—Find $\sqrt[3]{2·86}$, $\sqrt[3]{28·6}$ and $\sqrt[3]{286}$.

Set cursor to 2·86 on A and drawing the slide to the right find 1·42 under 1 on C, when 1·42 on B is under the cursor. Then reading under 1, $\sqrt[3]{10}$ and $\sqrt[3]{100}$, we have

$$\sqrt[3]{2·86}=1·42; \quad \sqrt[3]{28·6}=3·06 \text{ and } \sqrt[3]{286}=6·59.$$

It will be seen that factorising with powers of 10, we multiply the initial root by $\sqrt[3]{10}$ and $\sqrt[3]{100}$. Obviously the three roots will always be found on D, in their natural order and at intervals of one-third the length of the rule. The number of digits in the roots of numbers which do not lie between 1 and 1000, is found as before explained.

In any method of extracting cube roots in which the slide has to be adjusted to give equal readings on B and D, the author has found it of advantage to adopt the following plan.—The cursor being set to, say, 4·8 on A, bring a near *main* division line on B, as 1·7, to the cursor; then 1 on C is at 1·68 on D. The difference in the readings is two small divisions on D, and moving the slide forward by *one-third the space representing this difference*, we obtain 1·687 as the root required. With a little practice it is possible to obtain more accurate results by this method than by comparing the reading on D with that on the less finely-graded B scale.

---

* These lines should not be brought to the working edge of the scale but should terminate in the horizontal line which forms the border of the finer graduations, their value being read into the calculation by means of the cursor (see page 55).

MISCELLANEOUS POWERS AND ROOTS.

In addition to squares and cubes, certain other powers and roots may be readily obtained with the slide rule.

Two-thirds Power.—The value of $N^{\frac{2}{3}}$ is found on A over $\sqrt[3]{N}$ on D. The number of digits is decided by the rule for squares, working from the number of digits in the cube root. It will often be found preferable to treat $N^{\frac{2}{3}}$ as $N \div \sqrt[3]{N}$, as in this way the magnitude of the result is much more readily appreciated.

Three-two Power.—$N^{\frac{3}{2}}$ can be obtained by cubing the square root, deciding the number of digits in each process. For the reason just given, it is preferable to regard $N^{\frac{3}{2}}$ as $N \times \sqrt{N}$.

Fourth Power.—For N^4 set the index of C to N on D and over N on C read N^4 on A; or find the square of the square of N, deciding the number of digits at each step.

Fourth Root.—Similarly for $\sqrt[4]{N}$, take the square root of the square root.

Four-third Power.—$N^{\frac{4}{3}} = N^{1.33}$ (useful in gas-engine diagram calculations) is best treated as $N \times \sqrt[3]{N}$.

Other powers can be found by repeated multiplication. Thus setting 1 on B to N on A, we have on A, N^2 over N; N^3 over N^2; N^4 over N^3; N^5 over N^4, etc. In the same way, setting N on B to N on D, we can read such values as $N^{\frac{5}{2}}$, $N^{\frac{7}{2}}$, etc.

POWERS AND ROOTS BY LOGARITHMS.

For powers or roots other than those of the simple forms already discussed, it is necessary to employ the usual logarithmic process. Thus to find $a^n = x$, we multiply the logarithm of a by n, and find the number x corresponding to the logarithm so obtained. Similarly, to find $\sqrt[n]{a} = x$ we divide the logarithm of a by n, and find the number x corresponding to the resulting logarithm.

The Scale of Logarithms.—Upon the back of the slide of the Gravêt and similar slide rules there will be found three scales. One of these—usually the centre one—is divided equally throughout its entire length, and figured from right to left. It is sometimes marked L, indicating that it is a scale giving logarithms. The whole scale is divided primarily into ten equal parts, and each of these subdivided into 50 equal parts. In the recess or notch in the right-hand end of the rule is a reference mark, to which any of the divisions of this evenly-divided scale can be set.

As this decimally-divided scale is equal in length to the logarithmic scale D, and is figured in the reverse direction, it results that when the slide is drawn to the right so that the L.H. index of C coincides with any number on D, the reading on the equally-divided scale will give the decimal part of the logarithm of the number taken on D. Thus if the L.H. index of C is placed to agree with 2 on D, the reading of the back scale, taken at the reference mark, will be found to be 0·301, the logarithm of 2. It must be distinctly borne in mind that the number so obtained is the *decimal part* or *mantissa* of the logarithm of the number, and that to this the characteristic must be prefixed in accordance with the usual rule—viz., *The integral part, or characteristic of a logarithm is equal to the number of digits in the number, minus* 1. *If the number is wholly decimal, the characteristic is equal to the number of cyphers following the decimal point, plus* 1. In the latter case the characteristic is negative, and is so indicated by having the minus sign written *over* it.

To obtain any given power or root of a number, the operation is as follows:—Set the L.H. index of C to the given number on D, and turning the rule over, read opposite the mark in the notch at the right-hand end of the rule, the decimal part of the logarithm of the number. Add the characteristic according to the above rule, and multiply by the exponent of the power, or divide by the exponent of the root. Place the *decimal part* of the resultant reading, taken on the scale of equal parts, opposite the mark in the aperture of the rule, and read the answer on D under the L.H. index of C, pointing off the number of digits in the answer in accordance with the number of the characteristic of the resultant.

Ex.—Evaluate $36^{1\cdot414}$.

Set 1 on C to 36 on D and read the decimal part of log 36 on the scale of logarithms on the back of the slide. This value is found to be 0·556. As there are two digits in the number, the characteristic will be 1; hence log. 36 = 1·556. Multiply by 1·414, using the C and D scales, and obtain 2·2 as the log. of the result. Set the decimal part, 0·2, on the log. scale to the mark in the notch at the end of the rule and read 1585 on D under 1 on C. Since the log. of the result has a characteristic 2, there will be 3 digits in the result, which is therefore read as 158·5.

This example will suffice to show the method of obtaining the *n*th power or the *n*th root of *any* number.

OTHER METHODS OF OBTAINING POWERS AND ROOTS.

A SIMPLE method of obtaining powers and roots, which may serve on occasion, is by scaling off proportional lengths on the D scale (or the A scale) of the ordinary rule. Thus, to determine the value of $1\,25^{1\cdot67}$ we take the actual length 1-1·25 on D scale, and increase it by any convenient means in the proportion of $1:1\,67$. Then with a pair of dividers we set off this new length from 1, and obtain 1·44 as the result. One convenient method of obtaining the desired ratio is by a pair of proportional compasses. Thus to obtain $1\,52^{\frac{16}{17}}$, the compasses would be set in the ratio of 16 to 17, and the smaller end opened out to include 1-1·52 on the D scale; the opening in the large end of the compasses will then be such that setting it off from 1 we obtain 1·56 on D as the result sought.

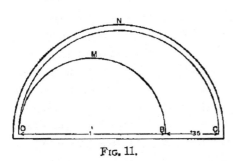

FIG. 11.

The converse procedure for obtaining the nth root of a number N will obviously resolve itself into obtaining $\frac{1}{n}$-th of the scale length 1-N, and need not be further considered.

Simple geometrical constructions are also used for obtaining scale lengths in the required ratio. A series of parallel lines ruled on transparent celluloid or stout tracing paper may be placed in an inclined position on the face of the rule and adjusted so as to divide the scale as desired. When much work is to be done which requires values to be raised to some constant but comparatively low power, n, the author has found the following device of assistance :—On a piece of thin transparent celluloid a line OC is drawn (Fig. 11) and in this a point B is taken such that $\frac{OC}{OB}$ is the desired ratio. It is convenient to make OB = 1 – 10 on the A scale, so that assuming we require a series of values of $v^{1\cdot 35}$, OB would be 12·5 cm. and OC, 16·875 cm. On these lines semi-circles are drawn as shown, both passing through the point O.

Applying this cursor to the upper scales so that the point O is on 1 and the semi-circle O M B passes through v on A, the larger semi-circle will give on A the value of v^n. Thus for $pv^n = 39.5 \times 4.9^{1.35}$, set 1 on B to 39·5 on A (Fig. 12) and apply the cursor to the working edge of B, so that O agrees with 1 and O M B passes through 4·9 on B. The larger semi-circle then cuts the edge of the slide on a point, giving 337 on A as the result required.

Of course any number of semi-circles may be drawn, giving different ratios. If a number of evenly-spaced divisions are used as bases, the device affords a simple means of obtaining a succession of small powers or roots, while it also finds a use in determining a number of geometric means between two values as is required in

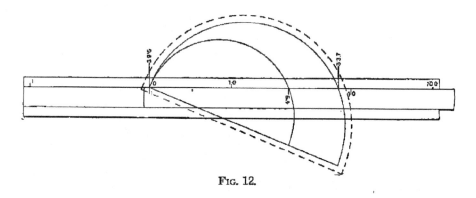

Fig. 12.

arranging the speed gears of machine tools, etc. The converse operation of finding roots will be evident as will also many other uses for which the device is of service.

The lines should be drawn in Indian ink with a very sharp pen and on the *under* side of the celluloid so that the lines lie in close contact with the face of the rule.

The Radial Cursor, another device for the same purpose, is always used in conjunction with the upper scales. As will be seen from Fig. 13, the body of the cursor P carries a graduated bar S which can be removed in a direction transverse to the rule, and adjusted to any desired position. Pivoted to the lower end of S is a radial arm R of transparent celluloid on which a centre line is engraved.

A reference to the illustration will show that the principle involved is that of similar triangles, the width of the slide being used as one of the elements. Thus, to take a simple case, if 2 on S is set to the index on P, and 1 on B is brought to N on A, then by swinging the radial arm until its centre line agrees with 1 on C, we can read N^2 on A. Evidently, since in the two similar triangles $A\,O\,N^2$ and $N\,t\,N^2$ the length of AO is twice that of Nt, it results that $A\,N^2 = 2\,A\,N$. In general, then, to find the nth power of a number, we set the cursor to 1 or 10 on A, bring n on the cross bar S to the index on the cursor, and 1 on B to N on A. Then to 1 on C we set the line on the radial arm, and under the latter read N^n on A. The inverse proceeding for finding the nth root will be obvious.

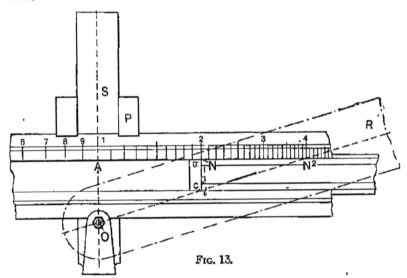

FIG. 13.

An advantage offered by this and analogous methods of obtaining powers and roots is that the result is obtained on the ordinary scale of the rule, and hence it can be taken directly into any further calculation which may be necessary.

COMBINED OPERATIONS.

THUS far the various operations have been separately considered, and we now pass on to a consideration of the methods of working for solving the various formulæ met with in technical calculations. We propose to explain the methods of dealing with a few of the more generally used expressions, as this will suffice to suggest the procedure in dealing with other and more intricate calculations. In solving the following problems, both the upper and lower scales are used, and the relative value of the several scales must be observed throughout. Thus, in solving such an expression as $\sqrt{\dfrac{745}{15\cdot 8}}=6\cdot 86$, the division is first effected by setting 15·8 on B to 745 on A. From the relation of the two parts of the upper scales (page 37) we know that such values as 7·45, 745, etc., will be taken on the *left-hand* A and B scales, while values as 15 8, 1580, etc., will be taken on the *right-hand* A and B scales. Hence, 15·8 on the R.H. B scale is set to 745 on the L.H. A scale, and the result read on D under the index of C. Had both values been taken on the L.H. A and B scales, or both on the R.H. A and B scales, the results would have corresponded to $x=\sqrt{\dfrac{7\cdot 45}{1\cdot 58}}=2\cdot 17$, or to $x=\sqrt{\dfrac{74\cdot 5}{15\cdot 8}}=2\cdot 17$, *i.e*, to $\dfrac{6\cdot 86}{\sqrt{10}}$. Hence if a wrong choice of scales has been made, we can correct the result by multiplying or dividing by $\sqrt{10}$ as the case may require. If the result is read on D, set to it the centre index (10) of B and read the corrected result under the index of C.

To solve $a\times b^2=x$. Set the index of C to b on D, and over a on B read x on A.

To solve $\dfrac{a^2}{b}=x$. Set b on B to a on D by using the cursor, and over index of B read x on A.

To solve $\dfrac{b}{a^2}=x$. Set a on C to b on A, and over 1 on B read x on A.

To solve $\dfrac{a\times b^2}{c}=x$. Set c on B to b on D, and over a on B read x on A.

To solve $(a\times b)^2=x$. Set 1 on C to a on D, and over b on C read x on A.

To solve $\left(\dfrac{a}{b}\right)^2=x$. Set b on C to a on D, and over 1 on C read x on A.

To solve $\sqrt{a\times b}=x$. Set 1 on B to a on A, and under b on B read x on D.

To solve $\sqrt{\dfrac{a}{b}}=x$. Set b on B on a on A, and under 1 on C read x on D.

To solve $a\dfrac{b}{c^2}=x$. Set b on C to c on D and over a on B read x on A.

To solve $c\sqrt{\dfrac{a}{b}}=x$. Set b on B to a on A, and under c on C read x on D.

To solve $\dfrac{\sqrt{a}}{b}=x$. Set b on C to a on A, and under 1 on C read x on D.

To solve $\dfrac{a}{\sqrt{b}}=x$. Set b on B to a on D, and under 1 on C read x on D.

To solve $b\sqrt{a}=x$. Set 1 on C to b on D, and under a on B read x on D.

To solve $\sqrt{a^3}=x$. Treat as $a\sqrt{a}$.

To solve $a\sqrt{b^3}=x$. Treat as $a\sqrt{b}\times b$.

To solve $\dfrac{\sqrt{a^3}}{b}=x$. Treat as $\dfrac{\sqrt{a}\times a}{b}$.

To solve $\sqrt{\dfrac{a^3}{b}}=x$. Treat as $\dfrac{\sqrt{a}\times a}{\sqrt{b}} = \sqrt{\dfrac{a}{b}}\times a$.

To solve $\sqrt{\dfrac{a\times b}{c}}=x$. Set c on B to a on A, and under b on B read x on D.

To solve $\dfrac{a\times b}{\sqrt{c}}=x$. Set c on B to b on D, and under a on C read x on D.

To solve $\sqrt{\dfrac{a^2\times b}{c}}=x$. Set c on B to a on D, and under b on B read x on D.

To solve $\dfrac{a^2\times b^2}{c}=x$. Set c on B to a on D, and over b on C read x on A.

To solve $\dfrac{a\sqrt{b}}{c}=x$. Set c on C to b on A, and under a on C read x on D.

To solve $\left(\dfrac{a\times\sqrt{b}}{c}\right)^2=x$. Set c on C to a on D, and over b on B read x on A.

HINTS ON EVALUATING EXPRESSIONS.

As a general rule, the use of cubes and higher powers should be avoided whenever possible. Thus, in the foregoing section, we recommend treating an expression of the form $a\sqrt{b^3}$ as $a \times b \times \sqrt{b}$; the magnitudes of the values thus met with are more easily appreciated by the beginner, and mistakes in estimating the large numbers involved in cubing are avoided.

Ex.—$7\cdot3 \times \sqrt{57^3} = 3140$.

Set 1 on C to 57 on D; bring cursor to 57 on B (R.H., since 57 has an *even* number of digits); bring 1 on C to cursor, and under $7\cdot3$ on C read 3140 on D. As a rough estimate we have $\sqrt{57}$, about 8; 8×57, about 400; 400×7, gives 2800, showing the result consists of 4 figures.

An expression of the form $a\sqrt[3]{b^2}$, or $ab^{\frac{2}{3}}$, is better dealt with by rearranging as $a \times \dfrac{b}{\sqrt[3]{b}}$.

Ex.—$3\cdot64 \sqrt[3]{4\cdot32^2} = 9\cdot65$.

Set cursor to $4\cdot32$ on A, and move the slide until $1\cdot63$ is found simultaneously under the cursor on B and on D under 1 on C; bring cursor to 1 on C; $4\cdot32$ on C to cursor, and *over* $3\cdot64$ on D read $9\cdot65$ on C. (Note that in this case it is convenient to read the answer on the *slide*; see page 22). From the slide rule we know $\sqrt[3]{4\cdot32}$ = about $1\cdot6$; this into $4\cdot32$ is roughly 3; $3\cdot64 \times 3$ is about 10, showing the answer to be $9\cdot65$.

Similarly products of the form $a \times b^{\frac{4}{3}}$ are best dealt with as $a \times b \times \sqrt[3]{b}$.

Factorising expressions sometimes simplifies matters, as, for instance, in $x^4 - y^4 = (x^2 + y^2)(x^2 - y^2)$. Here, working with the fourth powers involves large numbers and the troublesome determination of the number of digits in each factor; but squares are read on the rule at once, the number of digits is obvious, and, in general, the method should give a more accurate result. Take the expression, $D_1 = \sqrt[3]{\dfrac{D^4 - d^4}{D}}$ giving the diameter D_1 of a solid shaft equal in torsional strength to a hollow shaft whose external and internal diameters are D and d respectively. Rearranging as $D_1 = \sqrt[3]{\dfrac{(D^2 + d^2)(D^2 - d^2)}{D}}$ and taking, as an example, D=15 in.

and $d = 7$ in., we have $D^2 + d^2 = 274$ and $D^2 - d^2 = 176$; hence $D_1 = \sqrt[3]{\dfrac{274 \times 176}{15}} = \sqrt[3]{3210} = 14{\cdot}75$ in.

Reversed Scale Notation.—With expressions of the form $1-x$, or $100-x$, it is often convenient to regard the scales as having their notation reversed, *i.e.*, to read the scale backwards. When this is done the D scale is read as shown on the lower line—

Direct Notation	1	2	3	4	5	6	7	8	9	10
D Scale										
Reversed Notation	9	8	7	6	5	4	3	2	1	0

The new reading can be found by subtracting the ordinary reading from 1, 10, 100, etc., according to the value assigned to the R.H. index, but actually it is unnecessary to make this calculation, as with a little practice it is quite an easy matter to read both the main and subdivisions in the reversed order. Applications are found in plotting curves, trigonometrical formulæ, etc.

Ex.—Find the per cent. of slip of a screw propeller from
$$100 - S = \dfrac{10133\,V}{P\,R}$$
taking the speed, V, as 15 knots, the pitch of the propeller, P, as 27 ft. 6 in., and the revolutions per minute, R, as 60.

Set $27{\cdot}5$ on B to 10133 on A (N.B.—Take the setting near the *centre* index of A); bring the cursor to 15 on B and 60 on B to cursor. Reading the L.H. A scale backwards, the slip, S, $= 8$ per cent. is found on A over 10 on B.

Percentage Calculations.—To increase a quantity by x per cent. we multiply by $100+x$; to diminish a quantity by x per cent. we multiply by $100-x$. Hence, to add x per cent., set $100+x$ on C to 1 on D and read new values on D under original values on C. To deduct x per cent. read the D scale backwards from 10 and set R.H. index of C to x per cent. so read. Then read as before.

GAUGE POINTS.

SPECIAL graduations, marking the position of constant factors which frequently enter into engineering calculations, are found on most slide rules. Usually the values of $\pi = 3{\cdot}1416$ and $\dfrac{\pi}{4} = 0{\cdot}7854$—the "gauge points" for calculating the circumference and area of a circle—are marked on the upper scales. The first should be given on the lower scales also. Marks c and c^1 are sometimes found on the lower scales at $1{\cdot}128 = \sqrt{\dfrac{4}{\pi}}$ and at $3{\cdot}568 = \sqrt{\dfrac{40}{\pi}}$. These are useful in calculating the contents of cylinders and are thus derived:—Cubic contents of cylinder of diameter d and length $l = \dfrac{\pi}{4} d^2 l$; substituting for $\dfrac{\pi}{4}$ its reciprocal $\dfrac{4}{\pi}$, the formula becomes $\dfrac{d^2}{1{\cdot}273} \times l$, and by taking the square root of the fractional part we have $\left(\dfrac{d}{1{\cdot}128}\right)^2 \times l$. This is now in a very convenient form, since by setting the gauge point c on C to d on D, we can read over l on B the cubic contents on A. This example indicates the principle to be followed in arranging gauge points. Successive multiplication is avoided by substituting the reciprocal of the constant, thus bringing the expression into the form $\dfrac{a \times b}{c}$, which, as we know, can be resolved by one setting of the slide. The advantage of dividing d before squaring is also evident. The mark $c^1 = c \times \sqrt{10}$ is used if it is necessary to draw the slide more than one-half its length to the right.

A gauge point, M, at $31{\cdot}83 = \dfrac{100}{\pi}$ is found on the upper scales of some rules. Setting this point on B to the diameter of a cylinder on A, the circumference is read over 1 or 100 on B or the area of the curved surface over the length on B.

As another example of establishing a gauge point, we will take the formula for the theoretical delivery of pumps. If d is the diameter of the plunger in inches, l the length of stroke in feet, and Q the delivery in gallons, we have

$$Q = d^2 \times \dfrac{\pi}{4} \times l \times \dfrac{12}{277}.$$ (N.B.—277 cubic inches = 1 gallon.)

Multiplying out the constant quantities and taking its reciprocal, we readily transform the statement into $Q = \dfrac{d^2 l}{29{\cdot}4}$ or $\left(\dfrac{d}{5{\cdot}42}\right)^2 \times l$. Hence set gauge point $5{\cdot}42$ on C to d on D and over length of stroke in feet on B, read delivery in gallons per stroke on A; or over piston speed in feet per minute on B, read theoretical delivery in gallons per minute on A.

Several examples of gauge points will be found in the section on calculating the weights of metal (see pages 59 and 60). In most cases their derivation will be evident from what has been said above. In the case of the weight of spheres, we have Vol.= $0.5236\,d^3$, and this multiplied by the weight of 1 cubic inch of the material will give the weight W in lb. Hence for cast-iron, $W = 0.5236 \times d^3 \times 0.26$, which is conveniently transformed into $W = \dfrac{d \times d^2}{7.35}$ as in the example on page 60.

With these examples no difficulty should be experienced in establishing gauge points for any calculation in which constant factors recur.

Marking Gauge Points.—The practice of marking gauge points by lines extending to the working edge of the scale is not to be recommended, as it confuses the ordinary reading of the scales. Generally speaking, gauge points are only required occasionally, and if they are placed clear of the scale to which they pertain, but near enough to show the connection, they can be brought readily into a calculation by means of the cursor. Usually there is sufficient margin above the A scale and below the D scale for various gauge points to be marked. Another plan consists in cutting two nicks in the upper and lower edges of the cursor near the centre and about $\frac{1}{8}$ in. apart. These centre pieces, when bent out, form a tongue, which are in line with the cursor line and run nearly in contact with the square and bevelled edges of the rule respectively. A fine line in the tongue can then be set to gauge points marked on these two edge strips, the ordinary measuring graduations being removed, if desired, by a piece of fine sand-paper.

For gauge points marked on the face of the rule, the author prefers two fine lines drawn at 45°—thus, ✕—and crossing in the exact point which it is required to indicate. With the "cross" gauge point the meeting lines facilitate the placing of the cursor, and an exact setting is readily made.* All lines should be drawn in Indian ink with a very sharp drawing pen. For a more permanent marking the Indian ink may be rubbed up in glacial acetic acid or the special ink for celluloid may be used. If any difficulty is found in writing the distinguishing signs against the gauge point, the inscription may be formed by a succession of small dots made with a sharp pricker.

---

* The same principle may be applied to the cursor.

EXAMPLES IN TECHNICAL CALCULATIONS.

In order to illustrate the practical value of the slide rule, we now give a number of examples which will doubtless be sufficient to suggest the methods of working with other formulæ. A few of the rules give results which are approximate only, but in all cases the degree of accuracy obtained is well within the possible reading of the scales. In many cases the rules given may be modified, if desired, by varying the constants. In most of the examples the particular formula employed will be evident from the solution, but in a few of the more complicated cases a separate statement has been given.

Mensuration, Etc.

Given the chord c of a circular arc, and the vertical height h, to find the diameter d of the circle.

Set the height h on B to half the chord on D, and over 1 on B read x on A. Then $x + h = d$.

Ex.—$c = 6$; $h = 2$; find d.
Set 2 on B to 3 on D, and over 1 on B read 4·5 on A. Then $4·5 + 2 = 6·5 = d$.

Given the radius of a circle r, and the number of degrees n in an arc, to find the length l of the arc.

Set r on C to 57·3 on D, and over any number of degrees n on D read the (approximate) length of the arc on C.

Ex.—$r = 24$; $n = 30$; find l.
Set 24 on C to 57·3 on D, and over 30 on D read $12·56 = l$ on C.

Given the diameter d of a circle in *inches*, to find the circumference c in *feet*.

Set 191 on C to 50 on D, and under any diameter in inches on C read circumference c, in feet on D.

Ex.—Find the circumference in feet of a pulley 17in. in diameter.
Set 191 on C to 50 on D, and under 17 on C read 4·45ft. on D.

Given the diameter of a circle, to find its area.

Set 0·7854 on B to 10 (centre index) on A and over any diameter on D read area on B.

When the rule has a special graduation line $= 0·7854$, on the right-hand scale of B, set this line to the R.H index of A and read off as above. If only π is marked, set this special graduation on B to 4 on A.

On the C and D scales of some rules a gauge point marked c will be found indicating $\sqrt{\dfrac{4}{\pi}} = 1\cdot1286$. In this case, therefore, set 1 on C to gauge point c on D, and read area on A as above. If the gauge point c' is used, divide the result by 10. Or set c on C, to diameter on D, and over index of B read area on A. Cursors are supplied, having *two* lines ruled on the glass, the interval between them being equal to $\dfrac{4}{\pi} = 1\cdot273$ on the A scale. In this case, if the right hand of the two cursor lines be set to the diameter on D, the *area* will be read on A under the *left*-hand cursor line. For diameters less than 1·11 it is necessary to set the middle index of B to the L.H. index of A, reading the areas on the L.H. B scale. The confusion which in general work is sometimes caused by the use of two cursor lines might be obviated by making the left-hand line in two short lengths, each only just covering the scales.

Given diameter of circle d in *inches*, to find area a in square *feet*.

Set 6 on B to 11 on A, and over diameter in inches on D read area in square feet on B.

To find the surface in square feet of boiler flues, condenser tubes, heating pipes, etc., having given the diameter in inches and length in feet.

Find the circumference in feet as above and multiply by the length in feet.

Ex.—Find the heating surface afforded by 160 locomotive boiler tubes 1¾in. in diameter and 12ft. long

Set 191 on C to 50 on D; bring cursor 1·75 on C, L.H. index of C to cursor; cursor to 12 on C; 1 on C to cursor; and under 160 on C read 880 sq. ft. of heating surface on D.

If the dimensions are in the same denomination and the rule has a gauge point M at $31\cdot83\left(=\dfrac{100}{\pi}\right)$, set this mark on B to diameter of cylinder on A, and read cylindrical surface on A over length on B.

To find the side s of a square, equal in area to a given rectangle of length l and breadth b.

Set R.H. or L.H. index of B to l on A, and under b on B read s on D.

Ex.—Find the side of a square equal in area to a rectangle in which $l=31$ft. and $b=5$ft.

Set the (R.H.) index of B to 31 on A, and under 5 on B read 12·45ft. on D.

To find various lengths l and breadths b of a rectangle, to give a constant area a.

Invert the slide and set the index of C to the given area on D. Then opposite any length l on C find the corresponding breadth b on D.

Ex.—Find the corresponding breadths of rectangular sheets, 16, 18, 24, 36, and 60ft. long, to give a constant area of 72 sq. ft.

Set the R.H. index of C to 72 on D, and opposite 16, 18, 24, 36, and 60 on C read 4·5, 4, 3, 2, and 1·2ft., the corresponding breadths on D.

To find the contents in cubic feet of a cylinder of diameter d in inches and length l in feet.

Find area in feet as before, and multiply by the length.

If dimensions are all in inches or feet, set the mark c ($=1·128$) on C to diameter on D and over length on B, read cubic contents on A.

To find the area of an ellipse.

Set 205 on C to 161 on D; bring cursor to length of major axis on C, 1 on C to cursor, and under length of minor axis on C read area on D.

Ex.—Find the area of an ellipse the major and minor axes of which are 16in. and 12in. in length respectively.

Set 205 on C to 161 on D; bring cursor to 16 on C, 1 on C to cursor, and under 12 on C read 150·8in on D.

To find the surface of spheres.

Set 3·1416 on B to R.H. or L.H. index of A, and over diameter on D read by the aid of the cursor, the convex surface on B.

To find the cubic contents of spheres.

Set 1·91 on B to diameter on A, and over diameter on C read cubic contents on A.

WEIGHTS OF METALS.

To find the weight in lb. per lineal foot of square bars of metal.

Set index of B to weight of 12 cubic inches of the metal (*i.e.*, one lineal foot, 1 square inch in section) on A, and over the side of the square in inches on C read weight in lb. on A.

Ex.—Find the weight per foot length of 4½in. square wrought-iron bars.

Set middle index of B to 3·33 on A, and over 4½ on C read 67·5 lb. on A.

(N.B.—For other metals use the corresponding constant in column (2), below).

To find the weight in lb. per lineal foot of round bars.

Set R.H. or L.H. index of B to weight of 12 cylindrical inches of the metal on A (column (4), below), and opposite the diameter of the bar in inches on C, read weight in lb. per lineal foot on A.

Ex.—Find the weight of 1 lineal foot of 2in. round cast steel
Set L.H. index of B to 2·68 on A, and over 2 on C read 10·7lb. on A.

To find the weight of flat bars in lb. per lineal foot.

Set the breadth in inches on C to $\frac{1}{\text{weight of 12 cub. in.}}$ of the metal (column (3), below) on D, and above the thickness on D read weight in lb. per lineal foot on C.

Ex.—Find the weight per lineal foot of bar steel, 4½in. wide and ⅝in. thick.

Set 4·5 on C to 0·294 on D, and over 0·625 on D read 9·56lb. per lineal foot on C.

To find the weight per square foot of sheet metal, set the weight per cubic foot of the metal (col. 1) on C to 12 on D, and

Metals.	(1) Weight in lb. per cubic ft.	(2) Weight of 12 cubic in.	(3) $\frac{1}{\text{Wt. of 12 cub. in.}}$	(4) Weight of 12 cylindrical in.
Wrought iron...	480	3·33	0·300	2·62
Cast iron.........	450	3·125	0·320	2·45
Cast steel	490	3·40	0·294	2·68
Copper	550	3·82	0·262	3·00
Aluminium......	168	1·166	0·085	0·915
Brass	520	3·61	0·277	2·83
Lead	710	4·93	0·203	3·87
Tin	462	3·21	0·312	2·52
Zinc (cast)......	430	2·98	0·335	2·34
,, (sheet) .	450	3·125	0·320	2·45

above the thickness of the plate in inches on D read weight in lb. per square foot on C.

Ex.—Find the weight in lb. per square foot of aluminium sheet ⅜in. thick.

Set 168 on C to 12 on D, and over 0·375 on D read 5·25lb. on C.

To find the weight of pipes in lb. per lineal foot.

Set mean diameter of the pipe in inches (*i.e.*, internal diameter *plus* the thickness, or external diameter *minus* the thickness) on C to the constant given below on D, and over the thickness on D read weight in lb. per lineal foot on C.

Metals.	Constant for Pipes.	Constant for Spheres.
Wrought iron	0·0955	6·87
Cast iron	0·1020	7·35
Steel	0·0936	6·73
Brass	0·0882	6·35
Copper	0·0834	6·00
Lead	0·0646	4·65

Ex.—Find the weight per foot of cast-iron piping 4in. internal diameter and ½in. thick.

Set 4·5 on C to 0·102 on D, and over 0·5 on D read 22·1lb. on C, the required weight.

To find the weight in lb. of spheres or balls, given the diameter in inches. ($W = 0·5236\, d^3 \times$ wt. of 1 cub. in. of material).

Set the constant for spheres (given above) on B to diameter in inches on A, and over diameter on C read weight in lb. on A.

Ex.—Find the weight of a cast-iron ball 7½in. in diameter.

Set 7·35 on B to 7·5 on A, and over 7·5 on C read 57·7lb. on A.

To find diameter in inches of a sphere of given weight.

Set the cursor to the given weight in lb. on A, and move the slide until the same number is found on C under the cursor that is simultaneously found on A over the constant for the sphere on B.

Ex.—Find diameter in inches of a sphere of cast-iron to weigh 7½lb.

Setting the cursor to 7·5 on A, and moving the slide, it is found that when 3·8 on C falls under the cursor, 3·8 on A is simultaneously found over 7·35 on B. The required diameter is therefore 3·8in.

The rules for cubes and cube roots (page 40) should be kept in view in solving the last two examples.

Falling Bodies.

To find velocity in feet per second of a falling body, given the time of fall in seconds.

Set index on C to time of fall on D, and under 32·2 on C read velocity in feet per second on D.

To find velocity in feet per second, given distance fallen through in feet.

Set 1 on C to distance fallen through on A, and under 64·4 on B read velocity in feet per second on D.

Ex.—Find velocity acquired by falling through 14ft.

Set (R.H.) index of C to 14 on A, and under 64·4 on B read 30ft. per second on D.

To find distance fallen through in feet in a given time.

Set index of C to time in seconds on D, and over 16·1 on B read distance fallen through in feet on A.

Centrifugal Force.

To find the centrifugal force of a revolving mass in lb.

Set 2940 on B to revolutions per minute on D; bring cursor to weight in lb. on B; index of B to cursor, and over radius in feet on B read centrifugal force in lb. on A.

To find the centrifugal stress in lb per square inch, in rims of revolving wheels of cast iron.

Set 61·3 on C to the mean diameter of the wheel in feet on D, and over revolutions per minute on C read stress per square inch on A.

Ex.—Find the stress per square inch in a cast-iron fly-wheel rim 8ft. in diameter and running at 120 revolutions per minute.

Set 61·3 on C to 8 on D, and over 120 on C read 245lb. per square inch on A.

The Steam Engine.

Given the stroke and number of revolutions per minute, to find the piston speed.

Set stroke in inches on C to 6 on D, and over number of revolutions on D read piston speed in feet per minute on C.

To find cubic feet of steam in a cylinder at cut-off, given diameter of cylinder and period of admission in inches.

Set 2200 on B to cylinder diameter on D, and over period of admission on B read cubic feet of steam on A.

Ex.—Cylinder diameter 26in., stroke 40in., cut-off at ⅝ of stroke. Find cubic feet of steam used (theoretically) per stroke.

Set 2200 on B to 26 on D, and over 40 × ⅝ or 25in. on B, read 7·68 cub. ft. on A, as the number of cubic feet of steam used per stroke.

Given the diameter of a cylinder in inches, and the pressure in lb. per square inch, to find the load on the piston in tons.

Set pressure in lb. per square inch on B to 2852 on A, and over cylinder diameter in inches on D read load on piston in tons on B.

Ex.—Steam pressure 180lb. per square inch; cylinder diameter, 42in. Find load in tons on piston.

Set 180 on B to 2852 on A, and over 42 on D read 111 tons, the gross load, on B.

Given admission period and absolute initial pressure of steam in a cylinder, to find the pressure at various points in the expansion period (isothermal expansion).

Invert the slide and set the admission period, in inches, on C to the initial pressure on D; then under any point in the expansion stroke on C find the corresponding pressure on D.

Ex.—Admission period 12in., stroke 42in., initial pressure 80lb. per square inch. Find pressure at successive fifths of the expansion period.

Set 12 on C to 80 on D, and opposite 18, 24, 30, 36 and 42in. of the whole stroke on C find the corresponding pressures on D:—53·3, 40, 32, 26·6 and 22·8lb. per square inch.

To find the mean pressure constant for isothermally expanding steam, given the cut-off as a fraction of the stroke.

Find the logarithm of the ratio of the expansion r, by the method previously explained (page 46). Prefix the characteristic and to the number thus obtained, on D, set 1 on C. Then under 2·302 on C read x on D. To $x+1$ on D set r on C, and under index of C read mean pressure constant on D. The latter, multiplied by the initial pressure, gives the mean forward pressure throughout the stroke. (N.B.—Common log. × 2·302 = hyperbolic log.)

Ex.—Find the mean pressure constant for a cut-off of ¼th, or a ratio of expansion of 4.

Set (L.H.) index of C to 4 on D, and on the reverse side of the slide read 0·602 on the logarithmic scale. The characteristic = 0; hence to 0·602 on D set (R.H.) index of C, and under 2·302 on C read 1·384 on D. Add 1, and to 2·384 thus obtained on D set r (= 4) on C, and under 1 on C read 0·596, the mean pressure constant required.

Mean pressure constants for the most usual degrees of cut-off are given below:—

Cut-off in fractions of stroke...	$\frac{3}{4}$	$\frac{7}{10}$	$\frac{2}{3}$	$\frac{5}{8}$	$\frac{3}{5}$	$\frac{1}{2}$
Mean pressure constant.........	0·968	0·952	0·934	0·919	0·913	0·846
Cut-off in fractions of stroke...	$\frac{4}{9}$	$\frac{2}{5}$	$\frac{1}{3}$	$\frac{3}{10}$	$\frac{1}{4}$	$\frac{2}{9}$
Mean pressure constant.........	0·766	0·750	0·699	0·664	0·596	0·522
Cut-off in fractions of stroke...	$\frac{1}{5}$	$\frac{1}{6}$	$\frac{1}{7}$	$\frac{1}{8}$	$\frac{1}{9}$	$\frac{1}{10}$
Mean pressure constant.........	0·465	0·421	0·385	0·355	0·330	0·309
Cut-off in fractions of stroke...	$\frac{1}{12}$	$\frac{1}{13}$	$\frac{1}{14}$	$\frac{1}{15}$	$\frac{1}{16}$	
Mean pressure constant.........	0·290	0·274	0·260	0·247	0·236	

To find mean pressure:—Set 1 on C to constant on D, and under initial pressure on C read mean pressure on D.

Given the absolute initial pressure, length of stroke, and admission period, to find the absolute pressure at any point in the expansion period, it being assumed that the steam expands adiabatically. ($P_2 = \dfrac{P_1}{R^{\frac{10}{9}}}$ in which P_1=initial pressure and P_2 the pressure corresponding to a ratio of expansion R.)

Set L.H. index of C to ratio of expansion on D, and read on the back of the slide the decimal of the logarithm. Add the characteristic, and to the number thus obtained on D set 9 on C, and read off the value found on D under the index of C. Set this number on the logarithmic scale to the index mark, in the opening on the back of the rule, and under L.H. index of C read the value of $R^{\frac{10}{9}}$ on D. The initial pressure divided by this value gives the corresponding pressure due to the expansion.

Ex.—Absolute initial pressure 120lb. per square inch; stroke, 4ft.; cut-off $\frac{1}{4}$. Find the respective pressures when $\frac{1}{2}$ and $\frac{3}{4}$ths of the stroke have been completed.

In the first case R=2. Therefore setting the L.H. index of C to 2 on D, we find the decimal of the logarithm on the back of the slide to be 0·301. The characteristic is 0, so placing 9 on C to 0·301 on D, we read 0·334 as the value under the R.H. index of C. (N.B.—In locating the decimal point it is to be observed that the log. of R has been multiplied by 10, in accordance with the terms of the above expression.) Setting this number on the logarithmic scale to the back index, the value of $R^{\frac{10}{9}}$ is found on D, under the L.H. index of C, to be 2·16. Setting 120 on C to this value, it is found that the pressure at $\frac{1}{2}$ stroke, read on C over the R.H. index of D, is 55·5lb. per square inch. In a similar manner, the pressure when $\frac{3}{4}$ths of the stroke is completed is found to be 35·4lb. per square inch.

For other conditions of expanding steam, or for gas or air, the method of procedure is similar to the above.

E

To find the horse-power of an engine, having given the mean *effective* pressure, the cylinder diameter, stroke, and number of revolutions per minute.

To cylinder diameter on D set 145 on C; bring cursor to stroke in feet on B, 1 on B to cursor, cursor to number of revolutions on B, 1 on B to cursor, and over mean effective pressure on B find horse-power on A.

(N.B.—If stroke is in inches, use 502 in place of 145 given above.)

Ex.—Find the indicated horse-power, given cylinder diameter 27in., mean effective pressure 38lb. per square inch, stroke 32in., revolutions 57 per minute.

Set 502 on C to 27 on D, bring cursor to 32 on B, 1 on B to cursor, cursor to 57 on B, 1 on B to cursor, and over 38 on B read 200 I.H.P. on A.

To determine the horse-power of a compound engine, invert the slide and set the diameter of the *high*-pressure cylinder on C to the cut-off in that cylinder on A. Use the number then found on A over the diameter of the *low*-pressure cylinder on C as the cut-off in that cylinder, working with the same pressure and piston speed, and calculate the horse-power as for a single cylinder.

To find the cylinder ratio in compound engines, invert the slide and set index of C to diameter of the low-pressure cylinder on D. Then over the diameter of the high-pressure cylinder on C, read cylinder ratio on A.

Ex.—Diameter of high-pressure cylinder 7¾in., low-pressure 15in. Find cylinder ratio.

Set index on C to 15 on D, and over 7·75 on C read 3·75, the required ratio, on A.

The cylinder ratios of triple or quadruple-expansion engines may be similarly determined.

Ex.—In a quadruple-expansion engine, the cylinders are 18, 26, 37, and 54 inches in diameter. Find the respective ratios of the high, first intermediate, and second intermediate cylinders to the low-pressure.

Set (R.H.) index of C to 54 on D, and over 18, 26, and 37 on C read 9, 4·31, and 2·13, the required ratios, on A.

Given the mean effective pressures in lb. per square inch in each of the three cylinders of a triple-expansion engine, the I.H.P. to be developed in each cylinder, and the piston speed, to find the respective cylinder diameters.

Set 42,000 on B to piston speed on A; bring cursor to mean effective pressure in low-pressure cylinder on B, index of B to cursor, and under I.H.P. on A read low-pressure cylinder diameter on C. To find the diameters of the high-pressure and inter-mediate-pressure cylinders, invert the slide and place the mean pressure in the low-pressure cylinder on B to the diameter of that cylinder on D. Then under the respective mean pressures on B read corresponding cylinder diameters on D.

Ex.—The mean effective pressures in the cylinders of a triple-expansion engine are:—L.P., 10·32; I M.P., 27·5; and H.P., 77·5 lb. per square inch. The piston speed is 650ft. per minute, and the I.H.P. developed in each cylinder, 750. Find the cylinder diameters.

Set 42,000 on B to 650 on A, and bring cursor to 10·32 on B. Bring index of B to cursor, and under 750 on A read 68·5in. on C, the L.P cylinder diameter. Invert the slide, and placing 10·32 on B to 68·5 on D, read, under 27·5 on B, the I.M.P. cylinder diameter = 42in., on D; also under 77·5 on B read the H.P. cylinder diameter = 25in., on D.

To compute brake or dynamometrical horse-power.

Set 525 on C to the total weight in lb. acting at the end of the lever (or pull of spring balance in lb.) on D; set cursor to length of lever in feet on C, bring 1 on C to cursor, and under number of revolutions per minute on C find brake horse-power on D.

Given cylinder diameter and piston speed in feet per minute, to find diameter of steam pipe, assuming the maximum velocity of the steam to be 6000 ft. per minute.

Set 6000 on B to cylinder diameter on D, and under piston speed on B read steam pipe diameter on D.

Given the number of revolutions per minute of a Watt governor, to find the vertical height in inches, from the plane of revolution of the balls to the point of suspension.

Set revolutions per minute on C to 35,200 on A, and over index of B read height on A.

Given the weight in lb. of the rim of a cast-iron fly-wheel, to find the sectional area of the rim in square inches.

Set the mean diameter of the wheel in feet on C to 0·102 on D, and under weight of rim on C find area on D.

Given the consumption of coal in tons per week of 56 hours, and the I.H.P., to find the coal consumed per I.H.P. per hour.

Set I.H.P. on C to 40 on D, and under weekly consumption on C read lb. of coal per I.H.P., per hour on D.

Ex.—Find coal used per I.H.P. per hour, when 24 tons is the weekly consumption for 300 I.H.P.

Set 300 on C to 40 on D, and under 24 on C read 3·21lb. per I.H.P. per hour on D.

(N.B.—For any other number of working hours per week divide 2240 by the number of working hours, and use the quotient in place of 40 as above.)

To find the tractive force of a locomotive.

Set diameter of driving wheel in inches on B to diameter of cylinder in inches on D, and over the stroke in inches on B read on A, tractive force in lb. for each lb. of effective pressure on the piston.

STEAM BOILERS.

To find the bursting pressure of a cylindrical boiler shell, having given the diameter of shell and the thickness and ultimate strength of the material.

Set the diameter of the shell in inches on C to twice the thickness of the plate on D, and under strength of material per square inch on C read bursting pressure in lb. per square inch on D.

Ex.—Find the bursting pressure of a cylindrical boiler shell 7ft. 6in. in diameter, with plates ½-in. thick, assuming an ultimate strength of 50,000lb. per square inch.

Set 90 on C to 1·0 on D, and under 50,000 on C find 555lb. on D.

To find working pressure for Fox's corrugated furnaces by Board of Trade rule.

Set the least outside diameter in inches on C to 14,000 on D, and under thickness in inches on C read working pressure on D in lb. per square inch.

To find diameter d in inches, of round steel for safety valve springs by Board of Trade rule.

Set 8000 on C to load on spring in lb. on D, and under the mean diameter of the spring in inches on C read d^3 on D. Then extract the cube root as per rule.

SPEED RATIOS OF PULLEYS, ETC.

Given the diameter of a pulley and its number of revolutions per minute, to find the circumferential velocity of the pulley or the speed of ropes, belts, etc., driven thereby.

Set diameter of pulley in inches on C to 3·82 on D, and over revolutions per minute on D read speed in feet per minute on C.

Ex.—Find the speed of a belt driven by a pulley 53in. in diameter and running at 180 revolutions per minute.

Set 53 on C to 3·82 on D, and over 180 on D read 2500ft. per minute on C.

Ex.—Find the speed of the pitch line of a spur wheel 3ft. 6in. in diameter running at 60 revolutions per minute.

Set 42 in. on C to 3·82 on D, and over 60 on D read 660ft. per minute on C.

Given diameter and number of revolutions per minute of a driving pulley, and the diameter of the driven pulley, to find the number of revolutions of the latter.

Invert the slide and set diameter of driving pulley on C to given number of its revolutions on D; then opposite diameter of any driven pulley on C read its number of revolutions on D.

Ex.—Diameter of driving pulley 10ft.; revolutions per minute 55; diameter of driven pulley 2ft. 9in. Find number of revolutions per minute of latter.

Set 10 on C to 55 on D, and opposite 2·75 on C read 200 revolutions on D.

BELTS AND ROPES.

To find the ratio of tensions in the two sides of a belt, given the coefficient of friction between belt and pulley μ and the number of degrees θ in the arc of contact $\left(\log. R = \dfrac{\mu \theta}{132}\right)$.

Set 132 on C to the coefficient of friction on D, and read off the value found on D under the number of degrees in the arc of contact on C. Place this value on the scale of equal parts on the back of the slide, to the index mark in the aperture, and read the required ratio on D under the L.H. index of C.

Ex.—Find the tension ratio in a belt, assuming a coefficient of friction of 0·3 and an arc of contact of 120 degrees.

Set 132 on C to 0·3 on D, and under 120 on C read 0·273. Place this on the scale to the index on the back of the rule, and under the L.H. index C read 1·875 on D, the required ratio.

Given belt velocity and horse-power to be transmitted, to find the requisite width of belt, taking the effective tension at 50lb. per inch of width.

Set 660 on C to velocity in feet per minute on D, and opposite horse-power on D find width of belt in inches on C.

Given velocity and width of belt, to find horse-power transmitted.

Set 660 on C to velocity on D, and under width on C find horse-power transmitted on D.

(N.B.—For any other effective tension, instead of 660 use as a gauge point :—33,000 ÷ tension.)

Given speed and diameter of a cotton driving rope, to find power transmitted, disregarding centrifugal action, and assuming an effective working tension of 200lb. per square inch of rope.

Set 210 on B to 1·75 on D, and over speed in feet per minute on B read horse-power on A.

Ex.—Find the power transmitted by a 1¾in. rope running at 4000ft. per minute.

Set 210 on B to 1·75 on D, and over 4000 on B read 58·3 horse-power on A.

Find the "centrifugal tension" in the previous example, taking the weight per foot of the rope as $= 0.27 d^2$.

Set 655 on C to the diameter, 1·75in., on D, and over the speed, 4000ft. on C, read centrifugal tension = 114lb. on A.

Spur Wheels.

Given diameter and pitch of a spur wheel, to find number of teeth.

Set pitch on C to π (3·1416) on D, and under any diameter on C read number of teeth on D.

Given diameter and number of teeth in a spur wheel, to find the pitch.

Set diameter on C to number of teeth on D, and read pitch on C opposite 3·1416 on D.

Given the distance between the centres of a pair of spur wheels and the number of revolutions of each, to determine their diameters.

To twice the distance between the centres on D, set the sum of the number of revolutions on C, and under the revolutions of each wheel on C find the respective wheel diameters on D.

Ex.—The distance between the centres of two spur wheels is 37·5in., and they are required to make 21 and 24 revolutions in the same time. Find their respective diameters.

Set 21+24=45 on C to 75 (or 37·5 × 2) on D, and under 21 and 24 on C find 35 and 40in. on D as the respective diameters.

To find the power transmitted by toothed wheels, given the pitch diameter d in inches, the number of revolutions per minute n, and the pitch p in inches, by the rule, H.P. $= \dfrac{n d p^2}{400}$

Set 400 on B to pitch in inches on D; set cursor to d on B, 1 on B to cursor, and over any number of revolutions n on B read power transmitted on A.

Ex.—Find the horse-power capable of being transmitted by a spur wheel 7ft. in diameter, 3in. pitch, and running at 90 revolutions per minute.

Set 400 on B to 3 on D; bring cursor to 84in. on B, 1 on B to cursor, and over 90 revolutions on B read 170, the horse-power transmitted, on A.

Screw Cutting.

Given the number of threads per inch in the guide screw, to find the wheels to cut a screw of given pitch.

Set threads per inch in guide screw on C, to the number of threads per inch to be cut on D. Then opposite any number of teeth in the wheel on the mandrel on C, is the number of teeth in the wheel to be placed on the guide screw on D.

Strength of Shafting.

Given the diameter d of a steel shaft, and the number of revolutions per minute n, to find the horse-power from:—
$$\text{H.P.} = d^3 \times n \times 0\cdot02.$$

Set 1 on C to d on D, and bring cursor to d on B. Bring 50 on B to cursor, and over number of revolutions on B read H.P. on A.

Ex.—Find horse-power transmitted by a 3in. steel shaft at a 110 revolutions per minute.

Set 1 on C to 3 on D, and bring cursor to 3 on B. Bring 50 on B to cursor, and over 110 on B read 59·4 horse-power on A.

Given the horse-power to be transmitted and the number of revolutions of a steel shaft, to find the diameter.

Set revolutions on B to horse-power on A, and bring cursor to 50 on B. Then move the slide until the same number is found on B under the cursor that is simultaneously found on D under the index of C. This number is the diameter required.

To find the deflection k in inches, of a round steel shaft of diameter d, under a uniformly distributed load in lb. w, and supported by bearings, the centres of which are l feet apart
$$\left(k = \frac{w\, l^3}{78{,}000\, d^4} \right).$$

Modifying the form of this expression slightly, we proceed as follows:—Set d on C to l on D, and bring the cursor to the same number on B that is found on D under the index of C. Bring d on B to cursor, cursor to w on B, 78,800 on B to cursor, and read deflection on A over index of B.

Ex.—Find the deflection in inches of a round steel shaft 3½in. diameter, carrying a uniformly distributed load of 3200 lb., the distance apart of the centres of support being 9ft.

Set 3·5 on C to 9 on D, and read 2·57 on D, under the L.H. index of C. Set cursor to 2·57 on B, and bring 3·5 on B to cursor, cursor to 3200 on B, 78,000 on B to cursor, and over L.H. index of B read 0·199in., the required deflection on A.

To find the diameter of a shaft subject to twisting only, given the twisting moment in inch-lb. and the allowable stress in lb. per square inch.

Set the stress in lb. per square inch on B to the twisting moment in inch-lb. on A, and bring cursor to 5·1 on B. Then move the slide until the same number is found on B under the cursor that is simultaneously found on D under the index of C.

Ex.—A steel shaft is subjected to a twisting moment of 2,700,000 inch-lb. Determine the diameter if the allowable stress is taken at 9000 lb. per square inch.

Set 9000 on B to 2,700,000 on A, and bring the cursor to 5·1 on B. Moving the slide to the left, it is found that when 11·51 on the R.H. scale of B is under the cursor, the L.H. index of C is opposite 11·51 on D. This, then, is the required diameter of the shaft.

(N.B.—The rules for the scales to be used in finding the cube root (page 42) must be carefully observed in working these examples.)

Moments of Inertia.

To find the moment of inertia of a square section about an axis formed by one of its diagonals $\left(I = \dfrac{s^4}{12}\right)$.

Set index of C to the length of the side of square s on D; bring cursor to s on C, 12 on B to cursor, and over index of B read moment of inertia on A.

To find the moment of inertia of a rectangular section about an axis parallel to one side and perpendicular to the plane of bending.

Set index of C to the height or depth h of the section, and bring cursor to h on B. Set 12 on B to cursor, and over breadth b of the section on B read moment of inertia on A.

Ex.—Find the moment of inertia of a rectangular section of which $h = 14$ in. and $b = 7$ in.

Set index of C to 14 on D, and cursor to 14 on B. Bring 12 on B to cursor, and over 7 on B read 1600 on A.

Discharge from Pumps, Pipes, Etc.

To find the theoretical delivery of pumps, in gallons per stroke.

Set 29·4 on B to the diameter of the plunger in inches on D, and over length of stroke in feet on B read theoretical delivery in gallons per stroke on A.

(N.B.—A deduction of from 20 to 40 per cent. should be made to allow for slip.)

To find loss of head of water in feet due to friction in pipes (Prony's rule).

Set diameter of pipe in feet on B to velocity of water in feet per second on D and bring cursor to 2·25 on B; bring 1 on B to cursor, and over length of pipe in miles on B, read loss of head of water in feet, on A.

To find velocity in feet per second, of water in pipes (Blackwell's rule).

Set 2·3 on B to diameter of pipe in feet on A, and under inclination of pipe in feet per mile on B read velocity in feet per second on D.

To find the discharge over weirs in cubic feet per minute and per foot of width. (Discharge $= 214 \sqrt{h^3}$).

Set 0·00467 on C to the head in feet h on D, and under h on B read discharge on D.

To find the theoretical velocity of water flowing under a given head in feet.

Set index of B to head in feet on A, and under 64·4 on B read theoretical velocity in feet per second on D.

Horse-Power of Water Wheels.

To find the effective horse-power of a Poncelet water wheel.

Set 880 on C to cubic feet of flow of water per minute on D, and under height of fall in feet on C, read effective horse-power on D.

For breast water wheels use 960, and for overshot wheels 775, in place of 880 as above.

Electrical Engineering.

To find the resistance per mile, in ohms, of copper wire of high conductivity, at 60° F. the diameter being given in mils. (1 mil. = 0·001in.).

Set diameter of wire in mils. on C to 54,900 on A, and over R.H. or L.H. index of B read resistance in ohms on A.

Ex.—Find the resistance per mile of a copper wire 64 mils. in diameter.
Set 64 on C to 54,900 on A, and over R.H. index of B read 13·4 ohms on A.

To find the weight of copper wire in lb. per mile

Set 7·91 on C to diameter of wire in mils. on D, and over index of B read weight per mile on A.

Given electromotive force and current, to find electrical horse-power.

Set 746 on C to electromotive force in volts on D, and under current in ampères on C read electrical horse-power on D.

Given the resistance of a circuit in ohms and current in ampères, to find the energy absorbed in horse-power.

Set 746 on B to current on D, and over resistance on B read energy absorbed in H.P. on A.

Ex.—Find the H.P. expended in sending a current of 15 ampères through a circuit of 220 ohms resistance.
Set 746 on B to 15 on D, and over 220 on B read 66·3 H.P. on A.

COMMERCIAL.

To add on percentages.

Set 100 on C to 100+ given percentage on D, and under original number on C read result on D.

To deduct percentages.

Set R.H. index of C to 100− the given percentage on D, and under original number on C read result on D.

Ex.—From £16 deduct 7½ per cent.
Set 10 on C, to 92·5 on D and under 16 on C, read 14·8 = £14, 16s. on D.

To calculate simple interest.

Set 1 on C to rate per cent. on D; bring cursor to period on C and 1 on C to cursor. Then opposite any sum on C find simple interest on D.

For interest per annum.

Set R.H. index on C to rate on D, and opposite principal on C read interest on D.

Ex.—Find the amount with simple interest of £250 at 8 per cent., and for a period of 1 year and 9 months.
Set 1 on C to 8 on D; bring cursor to 1·75 on C, and 1 on C to cursor; then opposite 250 on C read £35, the interest, on D. Then 250 + 35 = £285 = the amount.

To calculate compound interest.

Set the L.H. index of C to the amount of £1 at the given rate of interest on D, and find the logarithm of this by reading on the reverse side of the rule, as explained on page 46. Multiply the logarithm, so found, by the period, and set the result, on the scale of equal parts, to the index on the under-side of the rule; then opposite any sum on C read the amount (including compound interest) on D.

Ex.—Find the amount of £500 at 5 per cent. for 6 years, with compound interest.

Set L.H. index of C to £1·05 on D, and read at the index on the scale of equal parts on the under side of rule, 0·0212. Multiply by 6, we obtain 0·1272, which, on the scale of equal parts, is placed to the index in the notch at the end of the rule. Then opposite 500 on C read £670 on D, the amount required, including compound interest.

MISCELLANEOUS CALCULATIONS.

To calculate percentages of compositions.

Set weight (or volume) of sample on C, to weight (or volume) of substance considered, on D; then under index of C read required percentage on D.

Ex.—A sample of coal weighing 1·25grms. contains 0·04425grm. of ash. Find the percentage of ash.

Set 1·25 on C to 0·04425 on D, and under index on C read 3·54, the required percentage of ash on D.

Given the steam pressure P and the diameter d in millimetres, of the throat of an injector, to find the weight W, of water delivered in lb. per hour from $W = \dfrac{d^2 \sqrt{P}}{0·505}$.

Set 0·505 on C to P on A; bring cursor to d on C and index of C to cursor. Then under d on C read delivery of water on D.

To find the pressure of wind per square foot, due to a given velocity in miles per hour.

Set 1 on B to 2 on A, and over the velocity in miles per hour on D read pressure in lb. per square foot on B.

To find the kinetic energy of a moving body.

Set 64·4 on B to velocity in feet per second on D, and over weight of body in lb. on B read kinetic energy or accumulated work in foot-lb. on A.

TRIGONOMETRICAL APPLICATIONS

Scales.—Not the least important feature of the modern slide rule is the provision of the special scales on the under-side of the slide, and by the use of which, in conjunction with the ordinary scales on the rule, a large variety of trigonometrical computations may be readily performed.

Three scales will be found on the reverse or under-side of the slide of the ordinary Gravêt or Mannheim rule. One of these is the evenly-divided scale or scale of equal parts referred to in previous sections, and by which, as explained, the decimal parts or mantissæ of logarithms of numbers may be obtained. Usually this scale is the centre one of the three, but in some rules it will be found occupying the lowest position, in which case some little modification of the following instructions will be necessary. The requisite transpositions will, however, be evident when the purposes of the scales are understood. The upper of the three scales, usually distinguished by the letter S, is a scale giving the logarithms of the sines of angles, and is used to determine the natural sines of angles of from 35 minutes to 90 degrees. The notation of this scale will be evident on inspection. The main divisions 1, 2, 3, etc., represent the degrees of angles; but the values of the subdivisions differ according to their position on the scale. Thus, if any primary space is subdivided into 12 parts, each of the latter will be read as 5 minutes (5'), since $1° = 60'$.

Sines of Angles.—To find the sine of an angle the slide is placed in the groove, with the under-side uppermost, and the end division lines or indices on the slide, coinciding with the right and left indices of the A scale. Then over the given angle on S is read the value of the sine of the angle on A. If the result is found on the left scale of A (1 to 10), the logarithmic characteristic is -2; if it is found on the right-hand side (10 to 100), it is -1. In other words, results on the right-hand scale are prefixed by the decimal point only, while those on the left-hand scale are to be preceded by a cypher also. Thus :—

$$\text{Sine } 2° \ 40' = 0.0465 \ ; \ \text{sine } 15° \ 40' = 0.270.$$

Multiplication and division of the sines of angles are performed in the same manner as ordinary calculations, excepting that the slide has its under-face placed uppermost, as just explained. Thus to multiply sine 15° 40′ by 15, the R.H. index of S is brought to 15 on A, and opposite 15° 40′ on S is found 4·05 on A. Again, to divide 142 by sine 16° 30′, we place 16° 30′ on S to 142 on A, and over R.H. index of S read 500 on A.

The rules for the number of integers in the results are thus determined: Let N be the number of integers in the multiplier M or in the dividend D. Then the number of integers P, in the product or Q, in the quotient are as follows :—

When the result is found to the right of M or D, and in the same scale	$P = N - 2$	$Q = N$
When the result is found to the right of M or D, and in the other scale	$P = N - 1$	$Q = N + 1$
When the result is found to the left of M or D, and in the other scale	$P = N - 1$	$Q = N + 1$
When the result is found to the left of M or D, and in the same scale	$P = N$	$Q = N + 2$

If the division is of the form $\dfrac{20° \, 30'}{50}$, the result cannot be read off directly on the face of the rule. Thus, if in the above example 20° 30′ on S, is placed to agree with 50 on the right-hand scale of A, the result found on S under the R.H. index of A is 44° 30′. The required numerical value can then be found: (1) By placing the slide with all indices coincident when opposite 44° 30′ on S will be found 0·007 on A; or (2) In the ordinary form of rule, by reading off on the scale B opposite the index mark in the opening on the under-side of the rule. The above rules for the number of integers in the quotient do not apply in this case.

If it is required to find the sine of an angle simply, this may be done with the slide in its ordinary position, with scale B under A. The given angle on scale S is then set to the index on the under-side of the rule, and the value of the sine is read off on B under the right index of A.

Owing to the rapidly diminishing differences of the values of the sines as the upper end of the scale is approached, the sines of angles between 60° and 90° cannot be accurately determined in the foregoing manner. It is therefore advisable to calculate the value of the sine by means of the formula:

$$\text{Sine } \theta = 1 - 2 \sin^2 \frac{90 - \theta}{2}.$$

To determine the value of $\sin^2 \frac{90-\theta}{2}$. With the slide in the normal position, set the value of $\frac{90-\theta}{2}$ on S to the index on the under-side of the rule, and read off the value x on B under the R.H. index of A. Without moving the slide find x on A, and read under it on B the value required.

Ex.—Find value of sine 79° 40'.

Sine 79° 40' = 1 − 2 sin² 5° 10'.

But sine 5° 10' = 0·0900, and under this value on A is 0·0081 on B. Therefore sine 79° 40' = 1 − 0·0162 = 0·9838.

The sines of very small angles, being very nearly proportional to the angles themselves, are found by direct reading. To facilitate this, some rules are provided with two marks, one of which, a single accent ('), corresponds to the logarithm of $\frac{1}{\text{sine } 1'}$ and is found at the number 3438. The other mark—a double accent (″)—corresponds to the logarithm of $\frac{1}{\text{sine } 1''}$ and is found at the number 206,265. In some rules these marks are found on either the A or the B scales; sometimes they are on both. In either case the angle on the one scale is placed so as to coincide with the significant mark on the other, and the result read off on the first-named scale opposite the index of the second.

In sines of angles under 3″, the number of integers in the result is −5; while it is −4 for angles from 3″ to 21″; −3 from 21″ to 3' 27″; and −2 from 3' 27″ to 34' 23″.

Ex.—Find sine 6'.

Placing the significant mark for minutes coincident with 6, the value opposite the index is found to be 175, and by the rule above this is to be read 0·00175. For angles in seconds the other significant mark is used; while angles expressed in minutes and seconds are to be first reduced to seconds. Thus, 3' 10″ = 190″.

Tangents of Angles.—There remains to be considered the third scale found on the back of the slide, and usually distinguished from the others by being lettered T. In most of the more recent forms of rule this scale is placed near the lower edge of the slide, but in some arrangements it is found to be the centre scale of the three. Again, in some rules this scale is figured in the same direction as the scale of sines—viz., from left to right,—while in others the T scale is reversed. In both cases there is now usually an aperture formed in the back of the left extremity of the rule, with an index mark similar to that already referred to in connection with the scale of sines. Considering what has been referred to as the more general arrangement, the method of determining the tangents of angles may be thus explained :—

The tangent scale will be found to commence, in some rules, at about 34', or, precisely, at the angle whose tangent is 0·01. More usually, however, the scale will be found to commence at about 5° 43', or at the angle whose tangent is 0·1. The other extremity of the scale corresponds in all cases to 45°, or the angle whose tangent is 1. This explanation will suggest the method of using the scale, however it may be arranged. If the graduations commence with 34', the T scale is to be used in conjunction with the right and left scales of A; while if they commence with 5° 43' it is to be used in conjunction with the D scale.

In the former case the slide is to be placed in the rule so that the T scale is adjacent to the A scales, and, with the right and left indices coinciding, when opposite any angle on T will be found its tangent on A. From what has been said above, it follows that the tangents read on the L.H. scale of A have values extending from 0·01 to 0·1; while those read on the R.H. scale of A have values from 0·1 to 1·0. Otherwise expressed, to the values of any tangent read on the L.H. scale of A a cypher is to be prefixed; while if found on the R.H. scale, it is read directly as a decimal.

Ex.—Find tan. 3° 50'.

Placing the slide as directed, the reading on A opposite 3° 50' on T is found to be 67. As this is found on the L.H. scale of A, it is to be read as 0·067.

Ex.—Find tan. 17° 45'.

Here the reading on A opposite 17° 45' on T is 32, and as it is found on the R.H. scale of A it is read on 0·32.

As in the case of the scale of sines, the tangents may be found without reversing the slide, when a fixed index is provided in the back of the rule for the T scale.

We revert now to a consideration of those rules in which a single tangent scale is provided. It will be understood that in this case the slide is placed so that the scale T is adjacent to the D scale, and that when the indices of both are placed in agreement, the value of the tangent of any angle on T (from 5° 43' to 45°) may be read off on D, the result so found being read as wholly decimal. Thus tan. 13° 20' is read 0·237.

If a back index is provided, the slide is used in its normal position, when, setting the angle on the tangent scale to this Index, the result can be read on C over the L.H. index of D.

The tangents of angles above 45° are obtained by the formula: Tan. $\theta = \dfrac{1}{\tan. (90-\theta)}$. For all angles from 45° to (90° − 5° 43') we proceed as follows:—Place (90 − θ) on T to the R.H. index of D, and read tan. θ on D under the L.H. index of T. The first figure in the value thus obtained is to be read as an integer. Thus, to find tan. 71° 20' we place 90° − 71° 20' = 18° 40' on T, to the R.H. index of D, and under the L.H. index of T read 2·96, the required tangent.

The tangents of angles less than 40' are sensibly proportional to the angles themselves, and as they may therefore be considered as sines, their value is determined by the aid of the single and double accent marks on the sine scale, as previously explained. The rules for the number of integers are the same as for the sines.

Multiplication and division of tangents may be quite readily effected.

Ex.—Tan. 21° 50' × 15 = 6.

Set L.H. index of T to 15 on D, and under 21° 50' on T read 6 on D.

Ex.—Tan. 72° 40' × 117 = 375.

Set (90° − 72° 40') = 17° 20' on T to 117 on D, and under R.H. index of T read 375 on D.

Cosines of Angles.—The cosines of angles may be determined by placing the scale S with its indices coinciding with those of A, and when opposite (90 − θ) on S is read cos. θ on A. If the result is read on the L.H. scale of A, a cypher is to be prefixed to the value read; while if it is read on the R.H. scale of A, the value is read directly as a decimal. Thus, to determine cos. 86° 30' we find opposite (90° − 86° 30') = 3° 30' on S, 61° on A, and as this is on the L.H. scale the result is read 0·061. Again, to find cos. 59° 20' we read opposite (90° − 59° 20′) or 30° 40′ on S, 51 on A, and as this is found on the R.H. scale of A, it is read 0·51.

In finding the cosines of small angles it will be seen that direct reading on the rule becomes impossible for angles of less than 20°. It is advisable in such cases to adopt the method described for determining the *sines* of the *large* angles of which the complements are sought.

Cotangents of Angles.—From the methods of finding the tangents of angles previously described, it will be apparent that the cotangents of angles may also be obtained with equal facility. For angles between 5° 45′ and 45°, the procedure is the same as that for finding tangents of angles greater than 45°. Thus, the angle on scale T is brought to the R.H. index of D, and the cotangent read off on D under the L.H. index of T. The first figure of the result so found is to be read as an integer.

If the angle (θ) lies between 45° and 84° 15′, the slide is placed so that the indices of T coincide with those of D, and the result is then read off on D opposite $(90 - \theta)$ on T. In this case the value is wholly decimal.

Secants of Angles.—The secants of angles are readily found by bringing $(90 - \theta)$ on S to the R.H. index of A and reading the result on A over the L.H. index of S. If the value is found on the L.H. scale of A, the first figure is to be read as an integer; while if the result is read on the R.H. scale of A, the first *two* figures are to be regarded as integers.

Cosecants of Angles.—The cosecants of angles are found by placing the angle on S to the R.H. index of A, and reading the value found on A over the L.H. index of S. If the result is read on the L.H. scale of A, the first figure is to be read as an integer; while if the result is found on the R.H. scale of A, the first *two* figures are to be read as integers.

It will be noted that some of the rules here given for determining the several trigonometrical functions of angles apply only to those forms of rules in which a single scale of tangents T is used, reading from left to right. For the other arrangements of the scale, previously referred to, some slight modification of the method of procedure in finding the tangents and cotangents of angles will be necessary; but as in each case the nature and extent of this modification is evident, no further directions are required.

THE SOLUTION OF RIGHT-ANGLED TRIANGLES.

From the foregoing explanation of the manner of determining the trigonometrical functions of angles, the methods of solving right-angled triangles will be readily perceived, and only a few examples need therefore be given.

Let a and b represent the sides and c the hypothenuse of a right-angled triangle, and $a°$ and $b°$ the angles opposite to the sides. Then of the possible cases we will take

(1.) Given c and $a°$, to find a, b, and $b°$.

The angle $b°=90-a°$, while $a=c \sin a°$ and $b=c \sin b°$. To find a, therefore, the index of S is set to c on A, and the value of a read on A opposite $a°$ on S. In the same manner the value of b is obtained.

Ex.—Given in a right-angled triangle $c=9$ ft. and $a°=30°$. Find a, b, and $b°$.

The angle $b°=90-30=60°$. To find a, set R.H. index of S to 9 on A, and over 30° on S read $a=4·5$ ft. on A. Also, with the slide in the same position, read $b=7·8$ ft. [7·794] on A over 60° on S.

(2.) Given a and c, to determine $a°$, $b°$, and b.

In this case advantage is taken of the fact that in every triangle the sides are proportional to the sines of the opposite angles. Therefore, as in this case the hypothenuse c subtends a right angle, of which the sine=1, the R.H. index (or 90°) on S is set to the length of c on A, when under a on A is found $a°$ on S. Hence $b°$ and b may be determined.

(3.) Given a and $a°$, to find b, c, and $b°$.

Here $b°=(90-a°)$, and the solution is similar to the foregoing.

(4.) Given a and b, to find $a°$, $b°$, and c.

To find $a°$, we have $\tan. a° = \dfrac{a}{b}$, which in the above example will be $\dfrac{4·5}{7·8}=0·577$. Therefore, placing the slide so that the indices of T coincide with those of D, we read opposite 0·577 on D the value of $a°=30°$. The hypothenuse c is readily obtained from $c = \dfrac{a}{\sin a°}$.

THE SOLUTION OF OBLIQUE-ANGLED TRIANGLES.

Using the same letters as before to designate the three sides and the subtending angles of oblique-angled triangles, we have the following cases:—

(1.) Given one side and two angles, as a, $a°$, and $b°$, to find b, c, and $c°$.

In the first place, $c° = 180° - (a° + b°)$; also we note that, as the sides are proportional to the sines of the opposite angles, $b = \dfrac{a \text{ sine } b°}{\text{sine } a°}$ and $c = \dfrac{a \text{ sine } c°}{\text{sine } a°}$.

Taking as an example, $a = 45$, $a° = 57°$, and $b° = 63°$, we have $c° = 180 - (57 + 63) = 60°$. To find b and c, set $a°$ on S to a on A, and read off on A above 63° and 60° the values of b ($= 47 \cdot 8$) and c ($= 46 \cdot 4$) respectively.

(2.) Given a, b, and $a°$, to find $b°$, $c°$, and c.

In this case the angle $a°$ on S is placed under the length of side a on A and under b on A is found the angle $b°$ on S. The angle $c° = 180 - (a° + b°)$, whence the length c can be read off on A over $c°$ on S.

(3.) Given the sides and the included angle, to find the other side and the remaining angles.

If, for example, there are given $a = 65$, $b = 42$, and the included angle $c° = 55°$, we have $(a + b) : (a - b) = \tan. \dfrac{a° + b°}{2} : \tan \dfrac{a° - b°}{2}$.

Then, since $a° + b° = 180° - 55° = 125°$, it follows that $\dfrac{a° + b°}{2} = \dfrac{125}{2} = 62° \, 30'$.

By the rule for tangents of angles greater than 45°, we find tan. $62° \, 30' = 1 \cdot 92$. Inserting in the above proportion the values thus found, we have $107 : 23 = 1 \cdot 92 : \tan. \dfrac{a° - b°}{2}$. From this it is found that the value of the tangent is $0 \cdot 412$, and placing the slide with all indices coinciding, it is seen that this value on D corresponds to an angle of $22° \, 25'$. Therefore, since $\dfrac{a° + b°}{2} = 62° \, 30'$, and $\dfrac{a° - b°}{2} = 22° \, 25'$, it follows that $a° = 84° \, 55'$, and $b° = 40° \, 5'$.

Finally, to determine the side c, we have $c = \dfrac{a \sin c°}{\sin a°}$ as before.

PRACTICAL TRIGONOMETRICAL APPLICATIONS.

A few examples illustrative of the application of the methods of determining the functions of angles, etc., described in the preceding section, will now be given.

To find the chord of an arc, having given the included angle and the radius.

With the slide placed in the rule with the C and D scales outward, bring one-half of the given angle on S to the index mark in the back of the rule, and read the chord on B under twice the radius on A.

Ex.—Required the chord of an arc of 15°, the radius being 23in.

Set 7° 30′ on S to the index mark in the back of the rule, and under 46 on A read 6in., the required length of chord on B.

To find the area of a triangle, given two sides and the included angle.

Set the angle on S to the index mark on the back of the rule, and bring cursor to 2 on B. Then bring the length of one side on B to cursor, cursor to 1 on B, the length of the other side on B to cursor, and read area on B under index of A.

Ex.—The sides of a triangle are 5 and 6ft. in length respectively, and they include an angle of 20°. Find the area.

Set 20 on S to index mark, bring cursor to 2 on B, 5 on B to cursor. cursor to 1 on B, 6 on B to cursor, and under 1 on A read the area = 5·13 sq ft. on B.

To find the number of degrees in a gradient, given the rise per cent.

Place the slide with the indices of T coincident with those of D, and over the rate per cent. on D read number of degrees in the slope on T.

As the arrangement of rule we have chiefly considered has only a single T scale, it will be seen that only solutions of the above problem involving slopes between 10 and 100 per cent. can be directly read off. For smaller angles, one of the formulæ for the determination of the tangents of sub-multiple angles must be used.

In rules having a double T scale (which is used with the A scale) the value in degrees of any slope from 1 to 100 per cent. can be directly read off on A.

To find the number of degrees, when the gradient is expressed as 1 in x.

Place the index of T to k on D, and over index of D read the required angle in degrees on T.

Ex.—Find the number of degrees in a gradient of 1 in 3·8.

Set 1 on T to 3·8 on D, and over R.H. index of D read 14° 45′ on T.

Given the lap, the lead and the travel of an engine slide valve, to find the angle of advance.

Set (lap+lead) on B to half the travel of the valve on A, and read the angle of advance on S at the index mark on the back of the rule.

Ex.—Valve travel 4½in., lap 1in., lead $\tfrac{5}{16}$in. Find angle of advance.

Set $1\tfrac{5}{16} = 1·312$ on B to 2·25 on A, and read 35° 40′ on S opposite the index on the back of the rule.

Given the angular advance θ, the lap and the travel of a slide valve, to find the cut-off in percentage of the stroke.

Place the lap on B to half the travel of valve on A, and read on S the angle (the supplement of the *angle of the eccentric*) found opposite the index in the back of the rule. To this angle, add the angle of advance and deduct the sum from 180°, thus obtaining the *angle of the crank* at the point of cut-off. To the cosine of the supplement of this angle, add 1 and multiply the result by 50, obtaining the percentage of stroke completed when cut-off occurs.

Ex.—Given the angular advance = 35° 40′, the valve travel = 4½in., and the lap = 1in., find the angle of the crank at cut-off and the admission period expressed as a percentage of the stroke.

Set 1 on B to 2·25 on A, and read off on S opposite the index, the supplement of the angle of the eccentric = 26° 20′. Then 180° − (35° 40′ + 26° 20′) = 118° = the crank angle at the point of cut-off. Further, cos. 118° = cos. 62° = sin (90° − 62°) = sin 28°, and placing 28° on S to the back index, the cosine, read on B under R.H. index of A, is found to be 0·469. Adding 1 and placing the L.H. index of C to the result, 1·469, on D, we read off under 50 on C, the required period of admission = 73·4 per cent. on D.

The trigonometrical scales are useful for evaluating certain formulæ. Thus in the following expressions, if we find the angle a such that sin. $a = k$, we can write:—

$$\frac{k}{\sqrt{1-k^2}} = \tan. a \; ; \quad \frac{\sqrt{1-k^2}}{k} = \cot. a \; ; \quad \sqrt{1-k^2} = \cos. a \; ; \quad \text{etc.}$$

In the first expression, take $k = 0·298$. Place the slide with the sine scale outward and with its indices agreeing with the indices of the rule. Set the cursor to 0·298 on the (R.H.) scale of A, and read 17° 20′ on the sine scale as the angle required. Then under 17° 20′ on the tangent scale, read 0·312 on D as the result.

SLIDE RULES WITH LOG.-LOG. SCALES.

For occasional requirements, the method described on page 45 of determining powers and roots other than the square and cube, is quite satisfactory. When, however, a number of such calculations are to be made, the process may be simplified considerably by the use of what are known as *log.-log.*, *logo-log.*, or *logometric* scales, in conjunction with the ordinary scales of the rule. The principle involved will be understood from a consideration of those rules for logarithmic computation (page 8) which refer to powers and roots. From these it is seen that while for the multiplication and division of numbers we *add* their logarithms, for involution and evolution we require to *multiply* or *divide* the logarithms of the numbers by the exponent of the power or root as the case may be. Thus to find $3^{2\cdot3}$, we have (log. 3) × 2·3 = log. x, and by the ordinary method described on page 45 we should determine log. 3 by the aid of the scale L on the back of the slide, multiply this by 2·3 by using the C and D scales in the usual manner, transfer the result to scale L, and read the value of x on D under 1 on C. By the simpler method, first proposed by Dr. P. M. Roget,* the multiplication of log. 3 by 2·3 is effected in the same way as with any two ordinary factors—*i.e.*, by adding their logarithms and finding the number corresponding to the resulting logarithm. In this case we have log. (log. 3) + log. 2·3 = log. (log. x). The first of the three terms is obviously the *logarithm of the logarithm* of 3, the second is the simple logarithm of 2·3, and the third the *logarithm of the logarithm of* the answer. Hence, if we have a scale so graduated that the distances from the point of origin represent the logarithms of the logarithms (the log.-logs.) of the numbers engraved upon it, then by using this in conjunction with the ordinary scale of logarithms, we can effect the required multiplication in a manner which is both expeditious and convenient. Slightly varying arrangements of the log.-log. scale, sometimes referred to as the "P line," have been introduced from time to time, but latterly the increasing use of exponential formulæ in thermodynamic, electrical, and physical calculations has led to a revival of interest in Dr. Roget's invention, and various arrangements of rules with log.-log. scales are now available.

---

* Philosophical Transactions of the Royal Society, 1815.

The Davis Log.-Log. Rule.—In the rule introduced by Messrs. John Davis & Son Limited, Derby, the log.-log. scales are placed upon a separate slide—a plan which has the advantage of leaving the rule intact for all ordinary purposes, while providing a length of 40in. for the log.-log. scales.

In the 10in. Davis rule one face of the slide, marked E, has two log.-log. scales for numbers greater than unity, the lower extending from 1·07 to 2, and the upper continuing the graduations from 2 to 1000. On the reverse face of the slide, marked −E, are two log.-log. scales for numbers less than unity, the upper extending from 0·001 to 0·5, and the lower continuing the graduations from 0·5 to 0·933. Both sets of scales are used in conjunction *with the lower or D scale of the rule*, which is to be primarily regarded as running from 1 to 10, and constitutes a scale of exponents. In the 20in. rule the log.-log. scales are more extensive, and are used in conjunction with the upper or A scale of the rule (1 to 100); in what follows, however, the 10in. rule is more particularly referred to.

It has been explained that on the log.-log. scale the distance of any numbered graduation from the point of origin represents the log.-log. of the number. The point of origin will obviously be that graduation whose log.-log.=0. This is seen to be 10, since log. (log. 10)=log. 1=0. Hence, confining attention to the E scale, to locate the graduation 20, we have log. (log. 20)=log. 1·301= 0·11397, so that if the scale D is 25cm. long, the distance between 10 and 20 on the corresponding log.-log. scale would be 113·97÷4 =28·49mm. For numbers less than 10 the resulting log.-logs. will be negative, and the distances will be spaced off from the point of origin in a negative direction—*i.e.*, from right to left. Thus, to locate the graduation 5, we have

log. (log. 5)=log. 0·699=$\overline{1}$·844; *i.e.*, −1+0·844 or −0·156;

so that the graduation marked 5 would be placed 156÷4=39 mm. distant from 10 in a *negative* direction, and proceeding in a similar manner, the scale may be extended in either direction. In the −E scale, the notation runs in the reverse direction to that of the E scale, but in all other respects it is precisely analogous, the distance from the point of origin (0·1 in this case) to any graduation x representing log. [−log. x]. It follows that of the similarly situated graduations on the two scales, those on the −E scale are the *reciprocals* of those on the E scale. This may be readily verified by setting, say, 10 on E to (R.H.) 1 on D, when turning to the back of the rule we find 0·1 on −E agreeing with the index mark in the aperture at the right-hand extremity of the rule.

In using the log.-log scales it is important to observe (1) that the values engraved on the scale are definite and unalterable (*e.g.*, 1·2 can only be read as 1 2 and not as 120, 0·0012, etc., as with the ordinary scales); (2) that the upper portion of each scale should be regarded as forming a prolongation to the right of the lower portion; and (3) that immediately above any value on the lower portion of the scale is found the 10th power of that value on the upper portion of the scale. Keeping these points in view, if we set 1·1 on E to 1 on D we find over 2 on D the value of $1·1^2=1·21$ on E. Similarly, over 3 we find $1·1^3=1·331$, and so on. Then, reading across the slide, we have, over 2, the value of $1·1^2 \times 10 = 1·1^{20} = 6·73$, and over 3 we have $1·1^3 \times 10 = 1·1^{30} = 17·4$. Hence the rule:—
To find the value of x^n, set x on E to 1 on D, and over n on D read x^n on E.

With the slide set as above, the 8th, 9th, etc., powers of 1·1 cannot be read off; but it is seen that, according to (2) in the foregoing, the missing portion of the E scale is that part of the upper scale (2 to about 2·6) which is outside the rule to the left. Hence placing 1·1 to 10 on D, the 8th, 9th, etc., powers of 1·1 will be read off *on the upper part* of the E scale. In general, then,

If x on the *lower* line is set to 1 on D, then x^n is read directly on that line and x^{10n} on the upper line.

If x on the *upper* line is set to 1 on D, then x^n is read directly on that line and $x^{\frac{n}{10}}$ on the lower line.

If x on the *lower* line is set to 10 on D, then $x^{\frac{n}{10}}$ is read directly on that line and x^n on the upper line.

If x on the *upper* line is set to 10 on D, then $x^{\frac{n}{10}}$ is read directly on that line and $x^{\frac{n}{100}}$ on the lower line.

These rules are conveniently exhibited in the accompanying diagram (Fig. 14). They are equally applicable to both the E and −E scales of the 10in. rule, and include practically all the instruction required for determining the *n*th power or the *n*th root of a number. They do not apply directly to the 20in. rule, however, for here the relation of the lower and upper scales will be x^n and x^{100n}.

Ex.—Find $1\cdot 167^{2\cdot 56}$.

Set $1\cdot 167$ on E to 1 on D, and over $2\cdot 56$ on D read $1\cdot 485$ on E.

Ex.—Find $4\cdot 6^{1\cdot 61}$.

Set $4\cdot 6$ on upper E scale to 1 on D, and over $1\cdot 61$ on D read $11\cdot 7$ ($11\cdot 67$) on E.

Ex.—Find $1\cdot 4^{0\cdot 27}$ and $1\cdot 4^{2\cdot 7}$.

Set $1\cdot 4$ on E to 10 on D, and over $2\cdot 7$ on D read $1\cdot 095 = 1\cdot 4^{0\cdot 27}$ on lower E scale and $2\cdot 48 = 1\cdot 4^{2\cdot 7}$ on upper E scale.

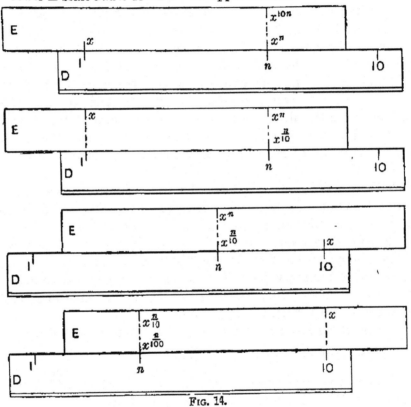

Fig. 14.

Ex.—Find $46^{0\cdot 0184}$ and $46^{0\cdot 184}$.

Set 46 on upper E scale to 10 on D, and over $1\cdot 84$ on D read $1\cdot 073$ on lower E scale and $2\cdot 022$ ($2\cdot 0223$) on upper E scale.

Ex.—Find $0\cdot 074^{1\cdot 15}$.

Using the $-$ E scale, set $0\cdot 074$ to 1 on D, and over $1\cdot 15$ on D read $0\cdot 05$ on $-$ E.

The method of determining the root of a number will be obvious from the preceding examples.

Ex.—Find $1\cdot 4\sqrt{17}$ and $14\sqrt{17}$.

Set 17 on E to $1\cdot 4$ on D, and over 1 on D read $7\cdot 56$ on upper E scale and $1\cdot 224$ on lower E scale.

Ex.—Find $^{0\cdot 031}\sqrt{0\cdot 914}$.

Set 0·914 on −E to 3·1 on D, and over 10 on D read 0·055 on upper −E scale.

When the exponent n is fractional, it is often possible to obtain the result directly with one setting of the slide. Thus to determine $1\cdot 135^{\frac{17}{16}}$ by the first method we find $\frac{17}{16} = 1\cdot 0625$, and placing 1·135 on E to 1 on D, read 1·144 on E over 1·0625 on D. By the direct method we place 1·135 on the E scale on 1·6 on D, and over 1·7 on D read 1·144 on E. It will be seen that since the scale D is assumed to run from 1 to 10 we are unable to read 16 and 17 on this scale; but it is obvious that the *ratios* $\frac{1\cdot 7}{1\cdot 6}$ and $\frac{17}{16}$ are identical, and it is with the ratio only that we are, in effect, concerned,

Since an expression of the form $x^{-n} = \frac{1}{x^n}$ or $\left(\frac{1}{x}\right)^n$, the required value may be obtained by first determining the reciprocal of x and proceeding as before. By using both the direct and reciprocal log.-log. scales (E and −E) in conjunction however, the required value can be read directly from the rule, and the preliminary calculation entirely avoided. In the Davis form of rule, the result can be read on the −E scale, used in conjunction with the D scale of the rule, x on E being set to the index mark in the aperture in the back of the rule.

Ex.—Find the value of $1\cdot 195^{-1\cdot 65}$.

Set 1·195 on E to the index in the left aperture in the back of the rule, and over 1·65 on D read 0·745 on the −E scale.

It may be noted in passing that the log.-log. scale affords a simple means for determining the logarithm or anti-logarithm of a number to any base. For this purpose it is necessary to set the base of the given system on E to 1 on D, when *under* any number on E will be found its logarithm on D. Thus, for common logs., we set the base 10 on E to 1 on D, and under 100 we find 2, the required log. Similarly we read log. 20 = 1·301; log. 55 = 1·74; log. 550 = 2·74, etc. Reading reversely, over 1·38 on D we find its antilog. 24 on E; also antilog. 1·58 = 38; antilog. 1·19 = 15·5, etc.

For logs. of numbers under 10 we set the base 10 to 10 on D; hence the readings on D will be read as one-tenth their apparent value. Thus log. 3 = 0·477; log. 5·25 = 0·72; antilog. 0·415 = 2·6; antilog. 0·525 = 3·35, etc.

The logs. of the numbers on the lower half of the E scale will also be found on the D scale; but a consideration of Fig. 14 will show that this will be read as *one-tenth* its face value if the base is set to 1 on D, and as *one-hundredth* if the base is set to 10.

For natural, hyperbolic, or Napierian logarithms, the base is $2 \cdot 718$. A special line marked ϵ or e serves to locate the exact position of this value on the E scale, and placing this to 1 on D we read $\log_e 4 \cdot 35 = 1 \cdot 47$; $\log_e 7 \cdot 4 = 2 \cdot 0$; antilog.$_e \times 2 \cdot 89 = 18$, etc. The other parts of the scale are read as already described for common logs. Calculations involving powers of e are frequently met with, and these are facilitated by using the special graduation line referred to, as will be readily understood.

If it is required to determine the power or root of a number which does not appear on either of the log.-log. scales, we may break up the number into factors. Usually it is convenient to make one of the factors a power of 10.

Ex.—$3950^{1 \cdot 97} = 3 \cdot 95^{1 \cdot 97} \times 10^{3 \times 1 \cdot 97} = 3 \cdot 95^{1 \cdot 97} \times 10^{5 \cdot 91}$.

Then $3 \cdot 95^{1 \cdot 97} = 15$, and $10^{5 \cdot 91}$ (or antilog.) $5 \cdot 91 = 812{,}000$. Hence, $15 \times 812{,}000 = 12{,}180{,}000$ is the result sought.

Numbers which are to be found in the higher part of the log.-log scale may often be factorised in this way, and greater accuracy obtained than by direct reading.

The form of log.-log. rule which has been mainly dealt with in the foregoing gives a scale of comparatively long range, and the only objection to the arrangement adopted is the use of a separate slide.

The Jackson-Davis Double Slide Rule.—In this instrument a pair of aluminium clips enable the log.-log. slide to be temporarily attached to the lower edge of the ordinary rule, and used, by means of a special cursor, in conjunction with the C scale of the ordinary slide. In this way both the log.-log. and ordinary scales are available without the trouble of replacing one slide by the other. Since the scale of exponents is now on the slide, the value of x^n will be obtained by setting 1 on C to x on E and reading the result on E under n on C.

By using a pair of log.-log. slides, one in the rule and one clamped to the edge by the clips, we have an arrangement which is very useful in deducing empirical formulæ of the type $y = x^n$.

The Yokota Slide Rule.—In this instrument the log.-log. scales are placed on the face of the rule, each set comprising three lines. These, for numbers greater than 1, are found above the A scale while the three reciprocal log.-log. lines are below the D scale. Both sets are used in conjunction with the C scale on the slide. Other features of this rule are :—The ordinary scales are 10in. long

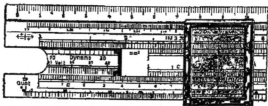

FIG. 15.

instead of 25cm. as hitherto usual ; hence the logarithms of numbers can be read on the ordinary scale of inches on the edge of the rule. There is a scale of cubes in the centre of the slide and on the back of the slide there is a scale of secants in addition to the sine and tangent scales.

The Faber Log.-log. Rule.—In this instrument shown in Fig. 15, the two log.-log. scales are placed on the face of the rule. One

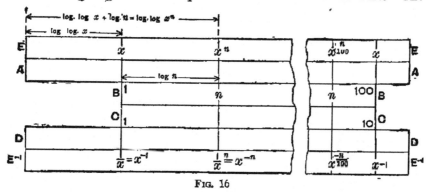

FIG. 16

section, extending from 1·1 to 2·9, is placed above the A scale, and the other section, extending from 2·9 to 100,000, is placed below the D scale. These scales are used in conjunction with the C scale of the slide in the manner previously described. The width of the rule is increased slightly, but the arrangement is more convenient than that formerly employed, wherein the log.-log. scales were placed on the bevelled edge of the rule and read by a tongue projecting from the cursor.

Another novel feature of this rule is the provision of two special scales at the bottom of the groove, to which a bevelled metal index or marker on the left end of the slide can be set. The upper of these scales is for determining the efficiency of dynamos and electric motors; the lower for determining the loss of potential in an electric circuit.

The Perry Log.-log. Rule.—In this rule, introduced by Messrs A. G. Thornton, Limited, Manchester, the log.-log. scales are arranged as in Fig. 16, the E scale, running from 1·1 to 10,000, being placed above the A scale of the rule, and the $-$E or E^{-1} scale running from 0·93 to 0·0001, below the D scale of the rule. These scales are read in conjunction with the B scales on the slide by the aid of the cursor.

The following tabular statement embodies all the instructions required for using this form of log.-log. slide rule :—

When x is greater than 1.

x^n Set 1 on B to x on E; over n on B read x^n on E.
x^{-n} Set 1 on B to x on E; under n on B read x^{-n} on E^{-1}.
$x^{\frac{1}{n}}$ Set n on B to x on E; over 1 on B read $x^{\frac{1}{n}}$ on E.
$x^{\frac{-1}{n}}$ Set n on B to x on E; under 1 on B read $x^{\frac{-1}{n}}$ on E^{-1}.

When x is less than 1.

x^n Set 1 on B to x on E^{-1}; under n on B read x^n on E^{-1}.
x^{-n} Set 1 on B to x on E^{-1}; over n on B read x^{-n} on E.
$x^{\frac{1}{n}}$ Set n on B to x on E^{-1}; under 1 on B read $x^{\frac{1}{n}}$ on E^{-1}.
$x^{\frac{-1}{n}}$ Set n on B to x on E^{-1}; over 1 on B read $x^{\frac{-1}{n}}$ on E.

If 10 on B is used in place of 1 on B, read $x^{\frac{n}{10}}$ in place of x^n on E, and $x^{\frac{-n}{10}}$ in place of x^{-n} on E^{-1}. If 100 on B is used, these readings are to be taken as $x^{\frac{n}{100}}$ and $x^{\frac{-n}{100}}$ respectively.

In rules with no $-$E scale the value of x^{-n} is obtained by the usual rules for reciprocals. We may either determine x^n and find its reciprocal or, first find the reciprocal of x and raise it to the nth power. The first method should be followed when the number x is found on the E scale.

Ex.—$3\cdot45^{-1\cdot82} = 0\cdot105$.

Set 1 on C to 3·45 on E, and under 1·82 on C read 9·51 on C. Then set 1 on B to 9·5 on A, and under index of A read 0·105 on B.

When x is less than 1 the second method is more suitable.

Ex.—$0 \cdot 23^{-1 \cdot 77} = \left(\dfrac{1}{0 \cdot 23}\right)^{1 \cdot 77} = 4 \cdot 35^{1 \cdot 77} = 13 \cdot 5$

Set 1 on B to 0·23 on A, and under index of A read $\dfrac{1}{0 \cdot 23} = 4 \cdot 35$ on B.

Set 1 on C to 4·35 on E, and under 1·77 on C read 13·5 on E.

As with the Davis rule, the exponent scale C will be read as $\frac{1}{10}$th its face value if its R.H. index (10) is used in place of 1.

SPECIAL TYPES OF SLIDE RULES.

IN addition to the new forms of log.-log. slide rules previously described, several other arrangements have been recently introduced, notably a series by Mr. A. Nestler, of Lahr (London: A. Fastlinger, Snow Hill). These comprise the "Rietz," the "Precision," the "Universal," and the "Fix" slide rules.

THE RIETZ RULE.—In this rule the usual scales A, B, C, and D, are provided, while at the upper edge is a scale, which, being three times the range of the D scale, enables cubes and cube roots to be directly evaluated and also $n^{\frac{2}{3}}$ and $n^{\frac{1}{3}}$.

A scale at the lower edge of the rule gives the mantissa of the logarithms of the numbers on D.

THE PRECISION SLIDE RULE.—In this rule the scales are so arranged that the accuracy of a 20in. rule is obtainable in a length of 10in. This is effected by dividing a 20in. (50cm.) scale length into two parts and placing these on the working edges of the rule and slide. On the upper and lower margins of the face of the rule are the two parts of what corresponds to the A scale in the ordinary rule; while in the centre of the slide is the scale of logarithms which, used in conjunction with the 50cm. scales on the slide, is virtually twice the length of that ordinarily obtainable in a 10in. rule. The same remark applies to the trigonometrical scales on the under face of the slide. Both the sine and tangent scales are in two adjacent lengths, while on the edge of the stock of the rule, below the cursor groove, is a scale of sines of small angles from 1° 49′ to 5° 44′. This is referred to the 50cm. scales by an index projection on the cursor.

If C and C′ are the two parts of the scale on the slide and D and D′ the corresponding scales on the rule, it is clear that in multiplying two factors 1 on C can only be set directly to the upper scale D; while 10 on C' can only be set directly to the lower scale D'. Hence if the first factor is greater than about 3·2, the cursor must be used to bring 1 on C to the first factor on D'. Similarly, in division, numerators and denominators which occur on C and D' or on C' and D cannot be placed in direct coincidence but must be set by the aid of the cursor.

Any uncertainty in reading the result can be avoided by observing the following rule: *If in setting the index (1 or 10) in multiplication, or in setting the numerator to the denominator in division, it is necessary to cross the slide, then it will also be necessary to cross the slide to read the product or quotient.*

THE UNIVERSAL SLIDE RULE.—In this instrument the stock carries two similar scales running from 1 to 10, to which the slide can be set. Above the upper one is the logarithm scale and under the lower one the scale of squares 1 to 100. On the edge of the stock of the rule, under the cursor groove, is a scale running from 1 to 1000. An index projecting from the cursor enables this scale to be used with the scales on the face of the rule, giving cubes, cube roots, etc.

On the slide, the lower scale is an ordinary scale, 1 to 10. The centre scale is the first part of a scale giving the values of sin n cos n, this scale being continued along the upper edge of the slide (marked "sin-cos") up to the graduation 50. On the remainder of this line is a scale running from right to left (0 to 50) and giving the value of $\cos^2 n$. In surveying, these scales greatly facilitate the calculations for the horizontal distance between the observer's station and any point, and the difference in height of these two points.

On the back of the slide are scales for the sines and tangents of angles. The values of the sines and tangents of angles from 34′ to 5° 44′ differ little from one another, and the one centre scale suffices for both functions of these small angles.

THE FIX SLIDE RULE.—This is a standard rule in all respects, except that the A scale is displaced by a distance $\frac{\pi}{4}$ so that over 1 on D is found 0·7854 on A. This enables calculations relating to the area and cubic contents of cylinders to be determined very readily.

THE BEGHIN SLIDE RULE.—We have seen that a disadvantage attending the use of the ordinary C and D scales, is that it is occasionally necessary to traverse the slide through its own length in order to change the indices or to bring other parts of the slide into a readable position with regard to the stock. To obviate this disadvantage, Tserepachinsky devised an ingenious arrangement which has since been used in various rules, notably in the Beghin slide rule made by Messrs. Tavernier-Gravêt of Paris. In this rule the C and D scales are used as in the standard rule, but in place of the A and B scales, we have another pair of C and D scales, displaced by one half the length of the rule. The lower pair of scales may therefore be regarded as running from 10^n to 10^{n+1}, and the upper pair as running from $\sqrt{10} \times 10^n$ to $\sqrt{10} \times 10^{n+1}$. With this arrangement, *without moving the slide more than half its length*, to the left or right, it is always possible to compare *all values between 1 and 10 on the two scales*. This is a great advantage especially in continuous working.

Another commendable feature of the Beghin rule is the presence of a reversed C scale in the centre of the slide, thus enabling such calculations as $a \times b \times c$ to be made with one setting of the slide. On the back of the slide are three scales, the lowest of which, used with the D scale, is a scale of squares (corresponding to the ordinary B scale), while on the upper edge is a scale of sines from 5° 44′ to 90°, and in the centre, a scale of tangents from 5° 43′ to 45°. On the square edge of the stock, under the cursor groove, is the logarithm scale, while on the same edge, above the cursor groove, are a series of gauge points. All these values are referred to the face scales by index marks on the cursor.

THE ANDERSON SLIDE RULE.—The principle of dividing a long scale into sections as in the Precision rule, has been extended in the Anderson slide rule made by Messrs. Casella & Co., London, and shown in Fig. 17. In this the slide carries a scale in four sections, used in conjunction with an exactly similar set of scale lines in the upper part of the stock. On the lower part of the stock is a scale in eight sections giving the square roots of the upper values. In order to set the index of the slide to values in the stock, two indices of transparent celluloid are fixed to the slide extending over the face of the rule as shown in the illustration. As each scale section is 30cm. in length, the upper lines correspond to a single scale of nearly 4ft., and the lower set to one of nearly 8ft. in length, giving a correspondingly large increase in the number of sub-divisions of these scales, and consequently much greater accuracy.

In order to decide upon which line a result is to be found, sets of "line numbers" are marked at each end of the rule and slide and also on the metal frame of the cursor. In multiplication, the line number of the product is the sum of the line numbers of the factors if the left index is used, or 1 more than this sum if the right index is used. The illustration shows the multiplication of 2 by 4. The left index is set to 2 (line number, 1), and the cursor set to 4 on the slide (line number, 2); hence, as the left index is used, the result is found on line No. 3. Similar rules are readily established for division. The column of line numbers headed 0 is used for units, that headed 4 for tens, and so on; one column is given for tenths, headed −4. The square root scale bears similar line numbers, so that the square root of any value on the upper scales is found on the correspondingly figured line below.

THE MULTIPLEX SLIDE RULE differs from the ordinary form of rule in the arrangement of the B scale. The right-hand section of this scale runs from left to right as ordinarily arranged, but the left-hand section runs in the reverse direction, and so furnishes a reciprocal scale. At the bottom of the groove, under the slide, there is a scale running from 1 to 1000, which is used in conjunction with the D scale, readings being referred thereto by a metal index on the end of the slide. By this means cubes, cube roots, etc., can be read off directly. Messrs. Eugene Dietzgen & Co., New York, are the makers.

FIG. 17.

The "Long" Slide Rule has one scale in two sections along the upper and lower parts of the stock, as in the "Precision" rule. The scale on the slide is similarly divided, but the graduations run in the reverse direction, corresponding to an inverted slide. Hence the rules for multiplication and division are the reverse of those usually followed (page 30). On the back of the slide is a single scale 1—10, and a scale 1—1000, giving cubes of this single scale. By using the first in conjunction with the scales on the stock, squares may be read, while in conjunction with the cube scale, various expressions involving squares, cubes and their roots may be evaluated.

Hall's Nautical Slide Rule consists of two slides fitting in grooves in the stock, and provided with eight scales, two on each slide, and one on each edge of each groove. While fulfilling the purposes of an ordinary slide rule, it is of especial service to the practical navigator in connection with such problems as the "reduction of an ex-meridian sight" and the "correction of chronometer sights for error in latitude." The rule, which has many other applications of a similar character, is made by Mr. J. H. Steward, Strand, London.

LONG-SCALE SLIDE RULES

It has been shown that the degree of accuracy attainable in slide-rule calculations depends upon the length of scale employed. Considerations of general convenience, however, render simple straight-scale rules of more than 20in. in length inadmissible, so that inventors of long-scale slide rules, in order to obtain a high degree of precision, combined with convenience in operation, have been compelled to modify the arrangement of scales usually employed. The principal methods adopted may be classed under three varieties: (1) The use of a long scale in sectional lengths, as in Hannyngton's Extended Slide Rule and Thacher's Calculating Instrument; (2) the employment of a long scale laid in spiral form upon a disc, as in Fearnley's Universal Calculator and Schuerman's Calculating Instrument; and (3) the adoption of a long scale wound helically upon a cylinder, of which Fuller's and the "R.H.S." Calculating Rules are examples.

Fuller's Calculating Rule.—This instrument, which is shown in Fig. 18, consists of a cylinder d capable of being moved up and down and around the cylindrical stock f, which is held by the handle. The logarithmic scale-line is arranged in the form of a helix upon the surface of the cylinder d, and as it is equivalent to a straight scale of 500 inches, or 41ft. 8in., it is possible to obtain four, and frequently five, figures in a result.

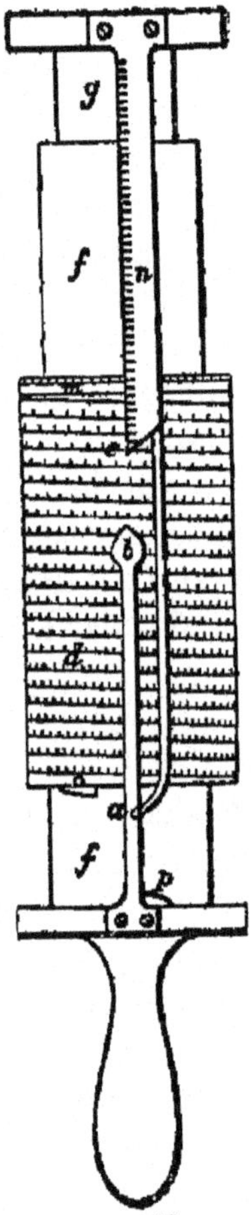

Upon reference to the figure it will be seen that three indices are employed. Of these, that lettered b is fixed to the handle; while two others, c and a (whose distance apart is equal to the axial length of the complete helix), are fixed to the innermost cylinder g. This latter cylinder slides telescopically in the stock f, enabling the indices to be placed in any required position relatively to d. Two other scales are provided, one (m) at the upper end of the cylinder d, and the other (n) on the movable index.

In using the instrument a given number on d is set to the fixed index b, and either a or c is brought to another number on the scale. This establishes a ratio, and if the cylinder is now moved so as to bring any number to b, the fourth term of the proportion will be found under a or c. Of course, in multiplication, one factor is brought to b, and a or c brought to 100. The other factor is then brought to a or c, and the result read off under b. Problems involving continuous multiplication, or combined multiplication and division, are very readily dealt with. Thus, calling the fixed index F, the upper movable index A, and the lower movable index B, we have for $a \times b \times c$.—Bring a to F; A to 100; b to A or B; A to 100; c to A or B and read the product at F.

Fig. 18

The maximum number of figures in a product is the sum of the number of figures in the factors and this results when all the factors except the first have to be brought to B. Each time a factor is brought to A, 1 is to be deducted from that sum.

For division, as $\frac{a}{m \times n}$, bring a to F; A or B to m; 100 to A; A or B to a; 100 to A and read the quotient at F.

The maximum number of figures in the quotient is the difference between the sum of the number of figures in the numerator factors and those of the denominator factors, *plus* 1 for each factor of the denominator and this results when A has to be set to all the factors of the denominator and all the factors of the numerator except the first brought to B. Each time B is set to a denominator factor or a numerator factor is brought to A, 1 is to be deducted.

Logarithms of numbers are obtained by using the scales m and n and hence powers and roots of any magnitude may be obtained by the procedure already fully explained. The instrument illustrated is made by Messrs. W. F. Stanley & Co., Limited, London.

The "R.H.S." Calculator.—In this calculator, designed by Prof. R. H. Smith, the scale-line, which is 50in. long, is also arranged in a spiral form (Fig. 19), but in this case it is wrapped around the central portion of a tube which is about ¾in. in diameter and 9½in. long. A slotted holder, capable of sliding upon the plain portions of this tube, is provided with four horns, these being formed at the ends of the two wide openings through which the scale is read. An outer ring carrying two horns completes the arrangement.

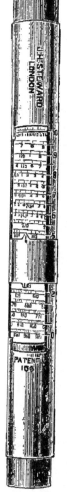

Fig. 19.

One of the horns of the holder being placed in agreement with the first factor, and one of the horns of the ring with the second factor, the holder is moved until the third factor falls under the same horn of the ring, when the resulting fourth term will be found under the same (right or left) horn of the holder, at either end of the slot. In multiplication, 100 or 1000 is taken for the second factor in the above proportion, as already explained in connection with Fuller's rule; indeed, generally, the mode of operation is essentially similar to that followed with the former instrument.

The scale shown on one edge of the opening in the holder, together with the circular scale at the top of the spiral, enables the mantissæ of logarithms of numbers to be obtained, and thus problems involving powers and roots may be dealt with quite readily. This instrument is supplied by Mr. J. H. Steward, London.

THACHER'S CALCULATING INSTRUMENT, shown in Fig. 20, consists of a cylinder 4in. in diameter and 18in. long, which can be given both a rotary and a longitudinal movement within an open framework composed of twenty triangular bars. These bars are connected to rings at their ends, which can be rotated in standards fixed to the baseboard. The scale on the cylinder consists of forty sectional lengths, but of each scale line that part which appears on

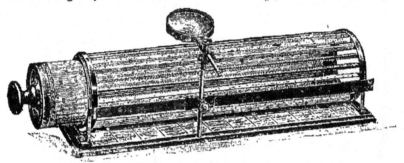

FIG. 20.

the right-hand half of the cylinder is repeated on the left-hand half, one line in advance. Hence each half of the cylinder virtually contains two complete scales following round in regular order. On the lower lines of the triangular bars are scales exactly corresponding to those on the cylinder, while upon the upper lines of the bars and not in contact with the slide is a scale of square roots.

By rotating the slide any line on it may be brought opposite any line in frame and by a longitudinal movement any graduation on these lines may be brought into agreement. The whole can be rotated in the supporting standards in order to bring any reading into view. As shown in the illustration, a magnifier is provided, this being conveniently mounted on a bar, along which it can be moved as required.

SECTIONAL LENGTH OR GRIDIRON SLIDE RULES.—The idea of breaking up a long scale into sectional lengths is due to Dr. J. D. Everett, who described such a gridiron type of slide rule in 1866.

Hannyngton's Extended Slide Rule is on the same principle. Both instruments have the lower scale repeated. H. Cherry (1880) appears to have been the first to show that such duplication could be avoided by providing two fixed index points in addition to the natural indices of the scale. These additional indices are shown at 10' and 100' in Fig. 21, which represents the lower sheet of Cherry's Calculator on a reduced scale. The upper member of the calculator consists of a transparent sheet ruled with parallel lines, which coincide with the lines of the lower scale when the indices of both are placed in agreement. To multiply one number by another, one of the indices on the upper sheet is placed to one of the factors, and the position of whichever index falls under the transparent

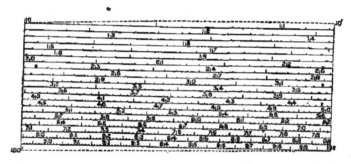

Fig. 21.

sheet is noted on the latter. Bringing the latter point to the other factor, the result is found under whichever index lies on the card. In other arrangements the inventor used transparent scales, the graduations running in a reverse direction to those of the lower scale. In this case, a factor on the upper scale is set to the other factor on the lower, and the result read at the available index.

Proell's Pocket Calculator is an application of the last-named principle. It comprises a lower card arranged as Fig. 21, with an upper sheet of transparent celluloid on which is a similar scale running in the reverse direction. For continued multiplication and division, a needle (supplied with the instrument) is used as a substitute for a cursor, to fix the position of the intermediate results. A series of index points on the lower card enable square and cube roots to be extracted very readily. This calculator is supplied by Messrs. John J. Griffin & Sons, Ltd., London.

CIRCULAR CALCULATORS.

ALTHOUGH the 10in. slide rule is probably the most serviceable form of calculating instrument for general purposes, many prefer the more portable circular-calculator, of which many varieties have been introduced during recent years. The advantages of this type are: It is more compact and conveniently carried in the waist-coat pocket. The scales are continuous, so that no traversing of the slide from 1 to 10 is required. The dial can be set quickly to any value; there is no trouble with tight or ill-fitting slides. The disadvantages of most forms are: Many problems involve more

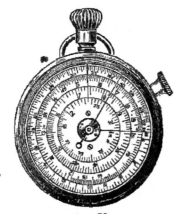

FIG. 22.

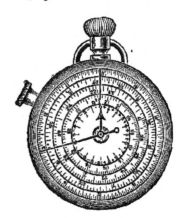

FIG. 23.

operations than a straight rule. The results being read under fingers or pointers, an error due to parallax is introduced, so that the results generally are not so accurate as with a straight rule. The inner scales are short, and therefore are read with less accuracy. Special scale circles are needed for cubes and cube roots. The slide cannot be reversed or inverted.

THE BOUCHER CALCULATOR.—This circular calculator resembles a stem-winding watch, being about 2in. in diameter and $\frac{9}{16}$in. in thickness. The instrument has two dials, the back one being fixed, while the front one, Fig. 22 (showing the form made by Messrs. W. F. Stanley, London), turns upon the large centre arbor shown. This movement is effected by turning the milled head of the stem-winder. The small centre axis, which is turned by rotating the milled head at the side of the case, carries two fine needle pointers, one moving over each dial, and so fixed on the axis that one pointer always lies evenly over the other. A fine index or pointer fixed to the case in line with the axis of the winding stem, extends over the four scales of the movable dial as shown. Of these scales, the second from the outer is the ordinary logarithmic scale, which in this instrument corresponds to a straight scale of about $4\tfrac{3}{4}$in. in length. The two inner circles give the square roots of the numbers on the primary logarithmic scale, the smaller circle containing the square roots of values between 1 and 3·162 ($=\sqrt{10}$), while the other section corresponds to values between 3·162 and 10. The outer circle is a scale of logarithms of sines of angles, the corresponding sines of which can be read off on the ordinary scale.

On the fixed or back dial there are also four scales, these being arranged as in Fig. 23. The outer of these is a scale of equal parts, while the three inner scales are separate sections of a scale giving the cube roots of the numbers taken on the ordinary logarithmic scale and referred thereto by means of the pointers. In dividing this cube-root scale into sections, the same method is adopted as in the case of the square-root scale. Thus, the smallest circle contains the cube roots of numbers between 1 and 10, and is therefore graduated from 1 to 2·154; the second circle contains the cube roots of numbers between 10 and 100, being graduated from 2·154 to 4·657; while the third section, in which are found the cube roots of numbers between 100 and 1000, carries the graduations from 4·657 to 10.

What has been said in an earlier section regarding the notation of the slide rule may in general be taken to apply to the scales of the Boucher calculator. The manner of using the instrument is, however, not quite so evident, although from what follows it will be seen that the operative principle—that of variously combining lengths of a logarithmic scale—is essentially similar. In this case, however, it is seen that in place of the straight scale-lengths shown in Fig. 4, we require to add or subtract arc-lengths of the circular scales, while, further, it is evident that in the absence of a fixed scale (corresponding to the stock of the slide rule) these operations cannot be directly performed as in the ordinary form of instrument. However, by the aid of the fixed index and the movable pointer, we can effect the desired combination of the scale-lengths in the following manner. Assuming it is desired to multiply 2 by 3, the dial is turned in a backward direction until 2 on the ordinary scale lies under the fixed index, after which the movable pointer is set to 1 on the scale. As now set, it is clear that the arc-length 1 – 2 is spaced-off between the fixed index and the movable pointer, and it now only remains to add to this definite arc-length a further length of 1 – 3. To do this we turn the dial still further backward until the arc 1 – 3 has passed under the movable pointer, when the result, 6, is read under the fixed index. A little consideration will show that any other scale-length may be added to that included between the fixed and movable pointers, or, in other words, any number on the scale may be multiplied by 2 by bringing the number to the movable pointer and reading the result under the fixed index. The rule for multiplication is now evident.

Rule for Multiplication.—*Set one factor to the fixed index and bring the pointer to 1 on the scale; set the other factor to the pointer and read the result under the fixed index.*

With the explanation just given, the process of division needs little explanation. It is clear that to divide 6 by 3, an arc-length 1 – 3 is to be taken from a length 1 – 6. To this end we set 6 to the index (corresponding in effect to passing a length 1 – 6 to the left of that reference point) and set the pointer to the divisor 3. As now set, the arc 1 – 6 is included between 1 on the scale and the index, while the arc 1 – 3 is included between 1 on the scale and the pointer. Obviously if the dial is now turned forward until 1 on the scale agrees with the pointer, an arc 1 – 3 will have been deducted from the larger arc 1 – 6, and the remainder, representing the result of this operation, will be read under the index as 2.

Rule for Division.—*Set the dividend to the fixed index, and the pointer to the divisor; turn the dial until 1 on the scale agrees with the pointer, and read the result under the fixed index.*

The foregoing method being an inversion of the rule for multiplication, is easily remembered and is generally advised. Another plan is, however, preferable when a series of divisions are to be effected with a constant divisor—*i.e.*, when b in $\frac{a}{b}=x$ is constant.

In this case 1 on the scale is set to the index and the pointer set to b; then if any value of a is brought to the pointer, the quotient x will be found under the index.

Combined Multiplication and Division, as $\frac{a \times b \times c}{m \times n} = x$, can be readily performed, while cases of continued multiplication evidently come under the same category, since $a \times b \times c = \frac{a \times b \times c}{1 \times 1} = x$. Such cases as $\frac{a}{m \times n \times r} = x$ are regarded as $\frac{a \times 1 \times 1 \times 1}{m \times n \times r} = x$; while $\frac{a \times b \times c}{m} = x$ is similarly modified, taking the form $\frac{a \times b \times c}{m \times 1} = x$. In all cases the expression must be arranged so that there is *one more factor in the numerator* than *in the denominator, 1's being introduced as often as required*. The simple operations of multiplication and division involve a similar disposition of factors, since from the rules given it is evident that $m \times n$ is actually regarded as $\frac{m \times n}{1}$, while $\frac{m}{n}$ becomes in effect $\frac{m \times 1}{n}$. It is important to note the general applicability of this arrangement-rule, as it will be found of great assistance in solving more complicated expressions.

As with the ordinary form of slide rule, the factors in such an expression as $\frac{a \times b \times c}{m \times n} = x$ are taken in the order:—1st factor of numerator; 1st factor of denominator; 2nd factor of numerator; 2nd factor of denominator, and so on; the 1st factor as a being set to the index, and the result x being finally read at the same point of reference.

Ex.—$\frac{39 \times 14\cdot2 \times 6\cdot3}{1\cdot37 \times 19} = 134$.

Commence by setting 39 to the index, and the pointer to 1·37; bring 14·2 to the pointer; pointer to 19; 6·3 to the pointer, and read the result 134 at the index.

It should be noted that after the first factor is set to the fixed index, the *pointer* is set to each of the *dividing* factors as they enter into the calculation, while the *dial* is moved for each of the *multiplying* factors. Thus the dial is first moved (setting the first factor to the index), then the pointer, then the dial, and so on.

Number of Digits in the Result.—If rules are preferred to the plan of roughly estimating the result, the general rules given on pages 21 and 25 should be employed for simple cases of multiplication and division. For combined multiplication and division, modify the expression, if necessary, by introducing 1's, as already explained, and subtract the sum of the denominator digits from the sum of numerator digits. Then proceed by the author's rule, as follows:—

Always turn dial to the LEFT; *i.e., against the hands of a watch.*

Note dial movements only; ignore those of the pointer.

Each time 1 on dial agrees with or passes fixed index, ADD 1 *to the above difference of digits.*

Each time 1 on dial agrees with or passes pointer, DEDUCT 1 *from the above difference of digits.*

Treat continued multiplication in the same way, counting the 1's used as denominator digits as one less than the number of multiplied factors.

$$\text{Ex.} - \frac{8 \cdot 6 \times 0 \cdot 73 \times 1 \cdot 02}{3 \cdot 5 \times 0 \cdot 23} = 7 \cdot 95 \; [7 \cdot 95473 +].$$

Set 8·6 to index and pointer to 3·5. Bring 0·73 to pointer (noting that 1 on the scale passes the index) and set pointer to 0·23. Set 1·02 to pointer (noting that 1 on the scale passes the pointer) and read under index 7·95. There are $1+0+1=2$ numerator digits and $1+0=1$ denominator digit; while 1 is to be added and 1 deducted as per rule. But as the latter cancel, the digits in the result will be $2-1=1$.

When moving the dial to the left will cause 1 on the dial to pass *both* index and pointer (thus cancelling), the dial may be turned back to make the setting.

It will be understood that when 1 is the *first* numerator, and 1 on the dial is therefore set to the index, no digit addition will be made for this, as the actual operation of calculating has not been commenced.

In the Stanley-Boucher calculator (Fig. 23) a small centre scale is added, on which a finger indicates automatically the number of digits to be added or deducted; the method of calculating, however, differs from the foregoing. To avoid turning back to 0 at the commencement of each calculation, a circle is ground on the glass face, so that a pencil mark can be made thereon to show the position of the finger when commencing a calculation.

To Find the Square of a Number.— Set the number, on one or other of the square root scales, to the index, and read the required square on the ordinary scale.

To Find the Square Root of a Number.—Set the number to the index, and if there is an *odd* number of digits in the number, read the root on the inner circle; if an even number, on the second circle.

To Find the Cube of a Number.—Set 1 on the ordinary scale to the index, and the pointer (on the back dial) to the number on one of the three cube-root scales. Then under the pointer read the cube on the ordinary scale.

To Find the Cube Root of a Number.—Set 1 to index, and pointer to number. Then read the cube root under the pointer on one of the three inner circles on the back dial. If the number has

1, 4, 7, 10 or −2, −5, etc., digits, use the inner circle.
2, 5, 8, 11 or −1, −4, etc.,   „   „   second circle.
3, 6, 9, 12 or −0, −3, etc.,   „   „   third circle.

For Powers or Roots of Higher Denomination.—Set 1 to index, the pointer to the number on the ordinary scale, and read on the outer circle on the back dial the mantissa of the logarithm. Add the characteristic (see p. 46), multiply by the power or divide by the root, and set the pointer to the mantissa of the result on this outer circle. Under the pointer on the ordinary scale read the number, obtaining the number of figures from the characteristic.

To Find the Sines of Angles.—Set 1 to index, pointer to the angle on the outer circle, and read under the pointer the *natural sine* on the ordinary scale; also under the pointer on the outer circle of the back dial read the *logarithmic sine*.

THE HALDEN CALCULEX.—After the introduction of the Boucher calculator in 1876, circular instruments, such as the Charpentier calculator, were introduced, in which a disc turned within a fixed ring, so that scales on the faces of both could be set together and ratios established as on the slide rule. Cultriss's Calculating Disc is another instrument on the same principle. The Halden Calculex, of which half-size illustrations are given in Figs. 24 and 25, represents a considerable improvement upon these early instruments. It consists of an outer metal ring carrying a fixed scale ring, within which is a dial. On each side of this dial are flat milled heads, so that by holding these between the thumb and forefinger the dial can be set quickly and conveniently. The protecting glass discs, which are not fixed in the metal ring but are arranged to turn therein, carry fine cursor lines, and as these are on the side next to the scales a very close setting can be made quite free from the effects of parallax. This construction not only avoids the use of mechanism, with its risk of derangement, but reduces the bulk of the instrument very considerably, the thickness being about ¼in.

On the front face, Fig. 24, the fixed ring carries an outer evenly-divided scale, giving logarithms, and an ordinary scale, 1—10, which works in conjunction with a similar scale on the edge of the dial. The two inner circles give the square roots of values on the main scales as in the Boucher calculator. On the back face, Fig. 25, the

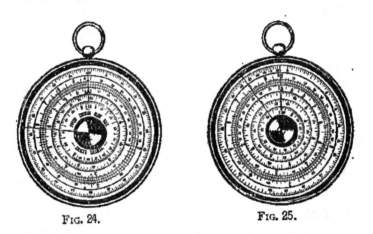

FIG. 24. FIG. 25.

ring bears an outer scale, giving sines of angles from 6° to 90° and an ordinary scale, 1—10, as on the front face. The scales on the dial are all reversed in direction (running from right to left), the outer one consisting of an ordinary (but inverse) scale, 1—10, while the three inner circles give the cube roots of values on this inverse scale. As the fine cursor lines extend over all the scales, a variety of calculations can be effected very readily and accurately.

SPERRY'S POCKET CALCULATOR, made by the Keuffel and Esser Company, New York (Fig. 26), has two rotating dials, each with its own pointer and fixed index. The S dial has an outer scale of equal parts, an ordinary logarithmic scale, and a square-root scale. The L dial has a single logarithmic scale arranged spirally, in three sections, giving a scale length of 12½in. The pointers are turned by the small milled head, which is concentric with the milled thumb-nut by which the two dials are rotated. The gearing

108   THE SLIDE RULE:

is such that both the L dial and its pointer rotate three times as fast as the S dial and pointer. All the usual calculations can be made with the spiral scale, as with the Boucher calculator, and the result read off on one or other of the three scale-sections. Frequently the point at which to read the result is obvious, but otherwise a reference to the single scale on the S dial will show on which of the three spirals the result is to be found.

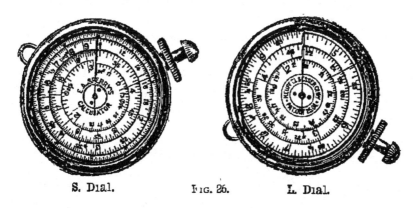

S. Dial.   Fig. 26.   L. Dial.

The K and E Calculator, also made by the Keuffel and Esser Company, is shown in Figs. 27 and 28. It has two dials, of which only one revolves. This, as shown in Fig. 27, has an ordinary

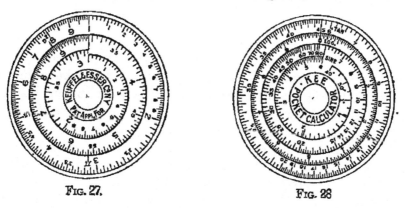

Fig. 27.   Fig. 28.

logarithmic scale and a scale of squares. There is an index line engraved on the glass of the instrument. The fixed dial has a scale of tangents, a scale of equal parts and a scale of sines, the latter being on a two-turn spiral. The pointers, which move together, are turned by a milled nut and the movable dial by a thumb-nut, as in Sperry's Calculator, Fig. 26.

SLIDE RULES FOR SPECIAL CALCULATIONS.

ENGINE POWER COMPUTER.—A typical example of special slide rules is shown in Fig. 29, which represents, on a scale of about half full size, the author's Power Computer for Steam, Gas, and Oil Engines. This, as will be seen, consists of a stock, on the lower portion of which is a scale of cylinder diameters, while the upper portion carries a scale of horse-powers. In the groove between these scales are two slides, also carrying scales, and capable of sliding in edge contact with the stock and with each other.

This instrument gives directly the brake horse-power of any steam, gas, or oil engine; the indicated horse-power, the dimensions of an engine to develop a given power, and the mechanical efficiency of an engine. The calculation of piston speed, velocity ratios of

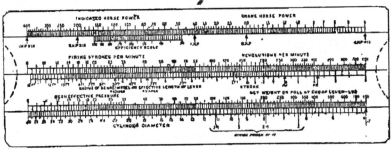

FIG. 29.

pulleys and gear wheels, the circumferential speed of pulleys, and the velocity of belts and ropes driven thereby, are among the other principal purposes for which the computer may be employed.

THE SMITH-DAVIS PIECEWORK BALANCE CALCULATOR has two scales, 11 feet long, having a range from 1d. to £20, and marked so that they can be used either for money or time calculations. The scales are placed on the rims of two similar wheels and so arranged that the divided edges come together. The wheels are mounted on a spindle carried at each end in the bearings of a supporting stand. The wheels are pressed together by a spring, and move as one.

To set the scales one to the other, a treadle gear is arranged to take the pressure of the spring so that when the fixed wheel is held by the left hand the free wheel can be rotated by the right hand in either direction. When the amount of the balance has been set to the combined weekly wage the treadle is released locking the two wheels together, when the whole can be turned and the amounts respectively due to each man read off opposite his weekly wage. The Smith-Davis Premium Calculator is on the same principle but the scales are about 4 feet 6 inches long and the wheels spring-controlled. Both instruments are supplied by Messrs. John Davis & Son, Ltd., Derby.

THE BAINES SLIDE RULE.—In this rule, invented by Mr. H. M. Baines, Lahore, four slides carrying scales are arranged to move, each in edge contact with the next. The slides are kept in contact and given the desired relative movement one to the other, by being attached (at the back), to a jointed parallelogram. On this principle which is of general application, the inventor has made a rule for the solution of problems covered by Flamant's formula for the flow of water in cast-iron pipes:—$V = 76\cdot28 d^{\frac{5}{7}} s^{\frac{4}{7}}$, in which s is the sine of the inclination or loss of head; d the diameter of the pipe in inches and V the velocity in feet per second. The formula $Q = AV$ is also included in the scope of the rule, Q being the discharge in cubic feet per second and A the cross sectional area of the pipe in square inches.

FARMAR'S PROFIT-CALCULATING RULE.—The application of the slide rule to commercial calculations has been often attempted, but the degree of accuracy required necessitates the use of a long scale, and generally this results in a cumbersome instrument. In Farmar's Profit-calculating Rule the money scale is arranged in ten sections, these being mounted in parallel form on a roller which takes the place of the upper scale of an ordinary rule. The roller, which is $\frac{3}{4}$-in. in diameter, is carried in brackets secured to each end of the stock, so that by rotating the roller any section of the money scale can be brought into reading with the scale on the upper edge of the slide and with which the roller is in contact. This scale gives percentages, and enables calculations to be made showing profit on turnover, profit on cost, and discount. The lower scale on the slide, and that on the stock adjacent to it, are similar to the A and B scales of an ordinary rule. The instrument is supplied by Messrs J. Casartelli & Son, Manchester.

CONSTRUCTIONAL IMPROVEMENTS IN SLIDE RULES.

THE attention of instrument makers is now being given to the devising of means for ensuring the smooth and even working of the slide in the stock of the rule. In some cases very good results are obtained by slitting the back of the stock to give more elasticity.

In the rules made by Messrs John Davis & Son, a metal strip, slightly curved in cross section as shown at A (Fig. 30), runs for the full length of the stock to which it is fastened at intervals. Near each end of the rule, openings about 1 in. long are made in the metal backing through which the scales on the back of the slide can be read. To prevent warping under varying climatic conditions both the stock of the rule and the slide are of composite construction. The base of the stock is of mahogany, while the grooved sides, firmly secured to the base, are of boxwood. Similarly the centre portion of the slide is of mahogany and the tongued sides of boxwood. Celluloid also enters into the construction, a strip of this

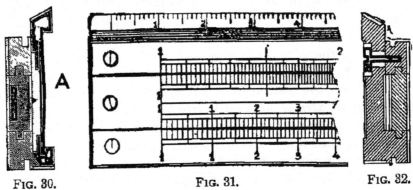

Fig. 30.   Fig. 31.   Fig. 32.

material being laid along the bottom of the groove in the stock. A fine groove runs along the centre of this strip in order to give elasticity, and to allow the sides of the stock to be pressed together slightly to adjust the fitting of the slide. As a further means of adjustment the makers fit metal clips at each end of the rule, so that by tightening two small screws the stock can be closed on the slide when necessary.

In the rule made by the Keuffel and Esser Company of New York, one strip is made adjustable (Fig. 32).

THE ACCURACY OF SLIDE RULE RESULTS.

The degree of accuracy obtainable with the slide rule depends primarily upon the length of the scale employed, but the accuracy of the graduations, the eyesight of the operator, and, in particular, his ability to estimate interpolated values, are all factors which affect the result. Using the lower scales and working carefully the error should not greatly exceed 0·15 per cent. with short calculations. With successive settings, the discrepancy need not necessarily be greater, as the errors may be neutralised; but with rapid working the percentage error may be doubled. However, much depends upon the graduation of the scales. Rules in which one or more of the indices have been thickened to conceal some slight inaccuracy should be avoided. The line on the cursor should be sharp and fine and both slide and cursor should move smoothly or good work cannot be done. Occasionally a little vaseline or clean tallow should be applied to the edges of the slide and cursor.

That the percentage error is constant throughout the scale is seen by setting 1 on C to 1·01 on D, when under 2 is 2·02; under 3, 3·03; under 5, 5·05, etc., the several readings showing a uniform error of 1 per cent.

A method of obtaining a closer reading of a first setting or of a result on D has been suggested to the author by Mr. M. Ainslie, B.Sc. If any graduation, as 4 on C, is set to 3 on D, it is seen that 4 main divisions on C (40-44) are equal in scale length to 3 main divisions on D (30-33). Hence, very approximately, 1 division on C is equal to 0·75 of a division on D, this ratio being shown, of course, on D under 10 on C. Suppose $\sqrt{4\cdot3}$ to be required. Setting the cursor to 4·3 on A, it is seen that the root is something more than 2·06. Move the slide until a main division is found on C, which exactly corresponds to the interval between 2 and the cursor line, on D. The division 27-28 just fits, giving a reading under 10 on C, of 74. Hence the root is read as 2·074. For the higher parts of the scale, the subdivisions, 1-1·1, etc., are used in place of main divisions. The method is probably more interesting than useful, since in most operations the inaccuracies introduced in making settings will impose a limit on the reliable figures of the result.

For the majority of engineering calculations, the slide rule will give an accuracy consistent with the accuracy of the data usually available. For some purposes, however, *logarithmic section paper* (the use of which the author has advocated for the last twenty years) will be found especially useful, more particularly in calculations involving exponential formulæ.

APPENDIX.

NEW SLIDE RULES—FIFTH ROOTS, ETC.—THE SOLUTION OF ALGEBRAIC EQUATIONS—GAUGE POINTS AND SIGNS ON SLIDE RULES—TABLES AND DATA—SLIDE RULE DATA SLIPS.

THE PICKWORTH SLIDE RULE.—In this rule, made by Mr A. W. Faber, the novel feature is the provision of a scale of cubes (F) in the stock or body of the rule. From Fig. 33 it will be seen that the scale is fixed on the bevelled side of a slotted recess in the back of the rule. The slide carries an index mark, which is seen through the slot and can be set to any graduation of the scale; in its normal position it agrees with 1 on the scale. The C scale on the face of

FIG. 33.

the rule is divided into three equal parts by two special division lines, marked II. and III., which, together with the initial graduation 1 of the scale, serve for setting or reading off values on the D scale. Similar division lines are marked on the D scale.

In using the rule for cubes or cube roots the slide is drawn to the right, this movement never exceeding one-third of the length of the D scale. With this limited movement, and with a single setting of the slide, the values of $\sqrt[3]{a}$, $\sqrt[3]{a \times 10}$, and $\sqrt[3]{a \times 100}$ (a being less than 10 and not less than 1) are given simultaneously and without any uncertainty as to the scales to use or the values to be read off.

To Find the Cube of a Number.—The marks II. and III. on D divide that scale into three equal sections. If the number to be cubed is in the first section, I. on C is set to it; if in the second section, II. on C is set to it; if in the third section, III. on C is set to it. Then, under the index mark on the back of the slide will be found the significant figures of the cube on the scale F. If I. on C was used for the setting, the cube contains 1 digit; if II. was used, 2 digits; if III. was used, 3 digits. If the first figure of the number to be cubed is not in the units place, the decimal point is moved through n places so as to bring the first significant figure into the units place, the cube found as above, and the decimal point moved in the *reverse direction* through $3n$ places.

To Find the Cube Root of a Number.—The index mark is set to the significant figures of the number on scale F, and the cube root is read on D under I., II. or III. on C, according as the number has 1, 2 or 3 digits preceding the decimal point. Numbers which have 1, 2 or 3 figures preceding the decimal point are dealt with directly. Numbers of any other form are brought to one of the above forms by moving the decimal point 3 places (or such multiple of 3 places as may be required), the root found and its decimal point moved 1 place for each 3-place movement, but in the *reverse direction*.

THE "ELECTRO" SLIDE RULE.—In this special rule for electrical calculations, made by Mr A. Nestler, the upper scales run from 0·1 to 1000, and are marked "Amp." and "sq. mm." respectively. The lower scale on the slide running from 1 to 10,000 is marked M (metres), while the lower scale on the rule (0·1 to 100) is marked "Volt." The latter scale is so displaced that 10 on M agrees with 0·173 on the Volt scale. The four factors involved are the current strength (in Amp.); the area of a conductor (in sq. mm.); the length of the conductor (in metres); and the permissible loss of potential (in volts). Having given any three of these, the fourth can be found very readily. On the back of the slide are a scale of squares, a scale of cubes and a single scale corresponding to the D scale of an ordinary rule. Hence, by reversing the slide, it is possible to obtain the 2nd, 3rd and 4th powers and roots of numbers. In another form of the rule, the scale of metres is replaced by one of yards, while instead of the area of the conductor in sq. mm., the corresponding "gauge" sizes of wires are given.

THE "POLYPHASE" SLIDE RULE.—This instrument, made by the Keuffel & Esser Company, New York, has, in addition to the usual scales, a scale of cubes on the vertical edge of the stock of the rule, while in the centre of the slide there is a reversed C scale; i.e., a scale exactly similar to an ordinary C scale but with the graduations running from right to left. The rule is specially useful for the solution of problems containing combinations of three factors and problems involving squares, square roots, cubes, cube roots and many of the higher powers and roots. It is specially adapted for electrical and hydraulic work.

THE LOG-LOG DUPLEX SLIDE RULE.—The same makers have introduced a log-log duplex slide rule, in which the log-log scale is in three sections, placed one above the other, these occupying the position usually taken up by the A scale. These scales are used in the manner already described (page 86), but some advantage is obtained by the manner in which the complete log-log scale is divided, the limits being $e^{\frac{1}{100}}$ to $e^{\frac{1}{10}}$ (on Scale L.L. 1); $e^{\frac{1}{10}}$ to e (on Scale L.L. 2); and e to e^{10} (on Scale L.L. 3), e being the base of natural or hyperbolic logarithms (2·71828). In this way a total log-log range of from 1·01 to 22,000 is provided, meeting all practical requirements. These log-log scales are read in conjunction with a C scale placed at the upper edge of the slide. A similar C scale, but reversed in direction, is placed at the lower edge of the slide, this having red figures to distinguish it readily. The adjacent scale on the body of the rule is an ordinary D scale, and under this is an equally-divided scale giving the common logarithms of values on D. In the centre of the slide is a scale of tangents.

It will be understood that a "duplex" rule consists of two side strips securely clamped together at the two ends, forming the body of the rule, the slide moving between them; hence both front and back faces of the rule and slide are available, graduations on the one side being referred to those on the other by the cursor which extends around the whole. In this instrument, the scales on the back face are the ordinary scales of the standard rule with the addition of a scale of sines which is placed in the centre of the slide. It will be evident that this instrument is capable of dealing with a very wide range of problems involving exponential and trigonometrical formulæ.

SMALL SLIDE RULES WITH MAGNIFYING CURSORS.—Several makers now supply 5-in. rules having the full graduations of a 10-in. rule, and fitted with a magnifying cursor (Fig. 34). This forms a compact instrument for the pocket, but owing to the closeness of the graduations it is not usually possible to make a setting of the slide without using the cursor. This, of course, involves more movements than with the ordinary instrument. It is also very necessary to use the magnifying cursor in a *direct* light, if accurate readings are to be obtained. If these slight inconveniences are to be tolerated, the principle could be extended, a 10-in. rule being marked as fully as a 20-in., and fitted with a magnifying cursor The author has endeavoured, but without success, to induce makers to introduce such a rule.

The magnifying cursor, supplied by Messrs A. G. Thornton, Limited, has a lens which fills the entire cursor. It has a powerful magnifying effect, and the change from the natural to the magnified reading is less abrupt than with the semicircular lens.

THE CHEMIST'S SLIDE RULE.—A slide rule, specially adapted for chemical calculations, has been introduced recently by Mr A.

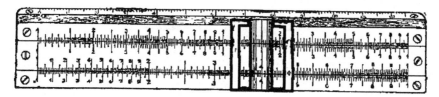

FIG. 34.

Nestler. In this instrument the C and D scales are as usually arranged; but, in place of the A and B scales, there are a number of gauge points or marks denoting the atomic and molecular weights of the most important elements and combinations. The scales on the back of the slide are similarly arranged, so that by reversing the slide the operations can be extended very considerably. The rule finds its chief use in the calculation of analyses. Thus, to find the percentage of chlorine if s grammes of a substance have been used and the precipitate of Ag Cl. weighs a grammes, we have the equation, $x \times \dfrac{Cl.}{Ag.\ Cl.} \times \dfrac{a}{s}$. Hence, the mark Ag. Cl. on the upper scale of the slide is set to the mark Cl. on the upper scale of the rule, when under a on the C scale is found the quantity of chlorine on D. By setting the cursor to this value and bringing s on C to the cursor, the percentage required can be read on C over 10 on D.

The rule is also adapted to the solution of various other chemical and electro-chemical calculations.

APPENDIX.

THE STELFOX SLIDE RULE.—This rule, shown in Fig. 35, has a stock 5 in. long, fitted with a 10-in. slide jointed in the middle of its length by means of long dowels. By separating the parts the compactness of a 5-in. rule is obtained. The upper scales on the rule and slide resemble the usual A and B scales. The D scale on the lower part of the stock is in two sections, the second portion being placed below the first, as shown in the illustration. The centre scale on the slide corresponds to the usual C scale, while on the lower edge of the slide is a similar scale, but with the index (1) in the middle of its length. The arrangement avoids the necessity of resetting the slide, as is sometimes necessary with the ordinary rule, and in general it combines the accuracy of a 10-in. rule with the compactness of a 5-in. rule; but a more frequent use of the cursor is necessary. This rule is made by Messrs John Davis & Son, Limited, Derby.

FIG. 35.

ELECTRICAL SLIDE RULE.—Another rule by the same makers, specially useful for electrical engineers, has the usual scales on the working edges of the rule and slide, while in the middle of the slide is placed a scale of cubes. A log-log scale in two sections is provided; the power portion, running from 1·07 to 2, is found on the lower part of the stock, and the upper portion, running from 2 to 10^8, on the upper part of the stock. The uppermost scale on the stock is in two parts, of which that to the left, running from 20 to 100 and marked "Dynamo," gives the efficiencies of dynamos; that on the right, running from 20 to 100 and marked "Motor," gives the efficiencies of electric motors. The lowest scale on the stock, marked "Volt," gives the loss of potential in copper conductors. The ordinary upper scale on the stock is marked L (length of lead) at the left, and KW (kilowatts) at the right; the ordinary upper scale on the slide is marked A (amperes) and mm^2 (sectional area) at the left, and HP (horse-power) at the right. Additional lines on the cursor enable the electrical calculations to be made either in British or metric units.

THE PICOLET CIRCULAR SLIDE RULE.—A simple form of circular calculator, made by Mr L. E. Picolet of Philadelphia, is shown in Fig. 36. It consists of a base disc of stout celluloid on which turns a smaller disc of thin celluloid. A cursor formed of transparent celluloid is folded over the discs, and is attached so that the friction between the cursor and the inner disc enables the latter to be turned by moving the former. By holding both discs the cursor can be adjusted as required. The adjacent scales run in opposite directions, so that multiplication and division are performed as with the inverted

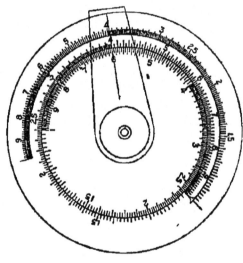

FIG 36.

slide in an ordinary rule. The outer scale, which is two-thirds the length of the main scale, enables cube roots to be found. Square roots are readily determined and continuous multiplication and division conveniently effected. Modified forms of this neatly made little instrument are also available.

OTHER RECENT SLIDE RULES.—Among other special types of slide rule, mention should be made of the *Jakin* 10-in. rule for surveyors, made by Messrs John Davis & Son, Limited, Derby. By the provision of a series of short subsidiary scales, the multiplication of a sine or tangent of an angle by a number can be obtained to an accuracy of 1 in 10,000. The *Davis-Lee-Bottomley* slide rule, by the same makers, has special scales provided for circle spacing. The division of a circle into a number of equal parts, often required

APPENDIX.

in spacing rivets, bolts, etc., and in setting out the teeth of gearwheels, is readily effected by the aid of this instrument. The *Cuntz* slide rule is a very comprehensive instrument, having a stock about $2\frac{1}{4}$ in. wide, with the slide near the lower edge. Above the slide are eleven scales, referable to the main scales by the cursor. These scales enable squares and square roots, cubes and cube roots, and areas and circumferences of circles to be obtained by direct reading. A much more compact instrument could be obtained by removing one-half the scales to the back of the rule and using a double cursor.

In one form of 10-in. rule, supplied by Mr W. H. Harling, London, the body of the rule is made of well-seasoned cane, with the usual celluloid facings. The rule has a metal back, enabling the fit of the

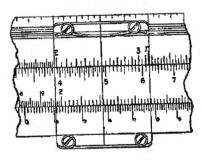

Fig. 37.

slide to be regulated. This backing extends the full length of the rule, openings about 1 in. long being provided at each end, enabling the scales on the back of the slide to be set with greater facility than is possible with the notched recesses usually adopted. The author has long endeavoured, but without success, to induce makers to fit windows of glass or celluloid in place of the notched recesses. This would allow the graduation of the S and T scales to be set more accurately, and enable both to be used at each end of the rule—an advantage in certain trigonometrical calculations. It would have the further advantage of permitting each alternate graduation of the evenly divided or logarithm scale to be placed at opposite sides of one central line, enabling the reading to be made more accurately and conveniently.

Many special slide rules have lately been devised for determining the time necessary to perform various machine-tool operations and for analogous purposes, while attention has again been given to rules for calculating the weights of iron and steel bars, plates, etc.

The Davis-Stokes Field Gunnery Slide Rule.—This rule, which is adapted for calculations involved in "encounter" and "entrenched" field gunnery, is designed for the 18 pr quick-firing gun. The upper and lower portions of the boxwood stock are united by a flexible centre of celluloid, thus providing grooves front and rear to receive boxwood slides. Each of the nineteen scales is marked with its name, and corresponding scales are coloured red or black. The front edge is bevelled and carries a scale of 1 in 20,000. The rule solves displacement problems, map angles of sight, changes of corrector and range corrections for changes in temperature, wind and barometer, etc. A special feature for displacement calculations is the provision of a 50-yd. sub-base angle scale, by which the apex angle is read at one setting.

The Davis-Martin Wireless Slide Rule.—In wireless telegraphy it is frequently necessary to determine wave-length, capacity or self-induction when one or other of the factors of the equation, $\lambda = 59\cdot6 \sqrt{LC}$ is unknown. The Davis-Martin wireless rule is designed to simplify such calculations. The upper scale in the stock (inductance) runs from 10,000 to 1,000,000; the adjacent scale on the slide (capacity) runs from 0·0001 to 0·01 but in the reverse direction. The lower scale on the stock (wave-length) runs from 100 to 1000, giving square roots of the upper scale; while on the lower edge of the scale are several arrows to suit the various denominations in which the wave-length and capacity may be expressed.

Improved Cursors.—In some slide-rule operations, notably in those involved in solving quadratic and cubic equations, it not infrequently happens that readings are obscured by the frame of the cursor. Frameless cursors have been introduced to obviate this defect. A piece of thick transparent celluloid is sometimes employed, but this is liable to become scratched in use. Fig. 37 shows a recent form of frameless glass cursor made by the Keuffel & Esser Company, Hoboken, N.J., which is satisfactory in every way.

Cursors having three hair lines are now fitted to some rules, the distance apart of the lines being equal to the interval $0\cdot7854 - 1$ on the A scale.

The Davis-Pletts Slide Rule.—In this rule a single log.-log scale and its reciprocal scale are arranged opposite the ordinary upper log. scale. Thus, common logarithms can be read directly, while by taking advantage of the properties of characteristics and mantissas of common logarithms, the scale can be extended indefinitely. As 10 is the highest number on the log.-log. scale, it is carried down to within 0·025 of unity. The reading of log.-log. values above 10 is effected in a very simple manner. There is also a scale in the centre of the slide which, used in conjunction with the upper log. scale enables the natural logarithm of any number between 0·0001 and 10,000 to be read direct, while any number on the upper log. scale can be multiplied or divided by e^x if the latter is between these limits. On the back of the slide are scales for all circular and hyperbolic functions, these being used in conjuction with the upper log. scales.

THE CROMPTON-GALLAGHER BOILER EFFICIENCY CALCULATOR has a stock in the thickness of which is a slot admitting a chart which can be moved at right angles to the two separate slides. On the bevelled edge of one slide, the graduations are continued so as to read against curves on the chart, through an opening in the stock

THE DAVIS-GRINSTED COMPLEX CALCULATOR.—This slide rule is of considerable service in connection with calculations involving the conversion of complex quantities from the form $a+jb$ to the form $R \angle \theta$, and *vice versa*. The usual process of conversion necessitates repeated reference to trigonometrical tables, and is both tedious and time-taking. The Complex Calculator enables the conversions to be effected without reference to tables and with the minimum expenditure of time and labour.

The rule, which is about 16 in. long, has five scales. The upper one (A) is an ordinary logarithmic scale thrice-repeated. The adjacent scales on the slide comprise (1) a logarithmic scale of tangents (B) ranging from 0·1° to 45°, and (2) a logarithmic scale of secants (C) from 0° to 45°. The lower scales D and E are identical with the A scale, and are provided to enable multiplication, etc., to be performed without the need for a separate slide rule. Readings can be transferred from A to the lower scales by means of the cursor.

In using the rule to convert $a+jb$ to $R \angle \theta$, the index (45°) of the B scale is set to the larger component and the cursor to the smaller component, on scale A. Then θ (or its complement if b is greater than a) is read on B under the cursor. The cursor is then set to θ on the C scale, and R is read on A under the cursor. The rule is made by Messrs. John Davis & Son, Limited, Derby.

THE SOLUTION OF ALGEBRAIC EQUATIONS.

The slide rule finds an interesting application in the solution of equations of the second and third degree; and although the process is essentially one of trial and error, it may often serve as an efficient substitute for the more laborious algebraic methods, particularly when the conditions of the problem or the operator's knowledge of the theory of equations enables some idea to be obtained as to the character of the result sought. The principle may be thus briefly explained:—If 1 on C is set to x on D (Fig. 38), we find $x(x) = x^2$ on D under x on C. If, however, with the slide set as before, instead of reading under x, we read under $x + m$ on C, the result on D will now be $x(x+m) = x^2 + mx = q$. Hence to solve the equation $x^2 + mx - q = 0$, we reverse the

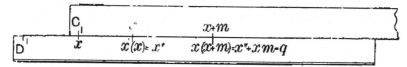

FIG. 38.

above process, and setting the cursor to q on D, we move the slide until the number on C under the cursor, and that on D under 1 on C, *differ by m*. It is obvious from the setting that the *product* of these numbers $= q$, and as their difference $= m$, they are seen to be the roots of the equation as required. For the equation $x^2 - mx + q = 0$, we require m to equal the *sum* of the roots. Hence, setting the cursor as before to q on D, we move the slide until the number on C under the cursor, and that on D under 1 on C, are *together equal to m*, these numbers being the roots sought. The alternative equations $x^2 - mx - q = 0$, and $x^2 + mx + q = 0$ are deducible from the others by changing the signs of the roots, and need not be further considered.

Ex.—Find the roots of $x^2 - 8x + 9 = 0$.

Set the cursor to 9 on D, and move the slide to the right until when 6·64 is found under the cursor, 1·355 on D is under 1 on C. These numbers are the roots required.

The upper scales can of course be used; indeed, in general they are to be preferred.

Ex.—Find the roots of $x^2 + 12·8x + 39·4 = 0$.

Set the cursor to 39·4 on A, and move the slide to the right until we read 7·65 on B under the cursor, and 5·15 on A over 1 on B. The roots are therefore $-7·65$ and $-5·15$.

APPENDIX.   123

With a little consideration of the relative value of the upper and lower scales, the student interested will readily perceive how equations of the third degree may be similarly resolved. The subject is not of sufficient general importance to warrant a detailed examination being made of the several expressions which can be dealt with in the manner suggested; but the author gives the following example as affording some indication of the adaptability of the method to practical calculations.

Ex.—A hollow copper ball, 7·5in. in diameter and 2lb. in weight, floats in water. To what depth will it sink?

The water displaced = 27·7 × 2 = 55·4 cub. in. The cubic contents of the immersed segment will be $\frac{\pi}{3}(3rx^2 - x^3)$, r being the radius and x the depth of immersion. Hence $\frac{\pi}{3}(3rx^2 - x^3) = 55·4$, and $11·25 x^2 - x^3 = 52·9$.

To solve this equation we place the cursor to 52·9 on A, and move the slide until the reading on D under 1 and that on B under the cursor together amount to 11·25. In this way find 2·45 on D under 1, with 8·8 on B under the cursor c, c, as a pair of values of which the sum is 11·25. Hence we conclude that $x = 2·45$in. is the result sought.

With the rule thus set (Fig. 39) the student will note that the slide is displaced to the right by an amount which represents x on D, and therefore x^2 on A; while the length on B from 1 to the

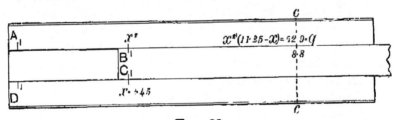

Fig. 39.

cursor line represents $11·25 - x$. Hence the upper scale setting gives $x^2(11·25 - x) = 11·25 x^2 - x^3 = 52·9$ as required.

When in doubt as to the method to be pursued in any given case, the student should work synthetically, building up a simple example of an analogous character to that under consideration, and so deducing the plan to be followed in the reverse process.

SCREW-CUTTING GEAR CALCULATIONS.

THE slide rule has long found a useful application in connection with the gear calculations necessary in screw-cutting, helical gear-cutting, and spiral gear work.

SINGLE GEARS.—For simple cases of screw-cutting in the lathe it is only necessary to set the threads per inch to be cut to the threads per inch in the guide screw (or the pitch in inches in each case, if more convenient). Then any pair of coinciding values on the two scales will give possible pairs of wheels.

Ex.—Find wheels to cut a screw of $1\frac{5}{8}$ threads per inch with a guide screw of 2 threads per inch.

Setting 1·625 on C to 2 on D, it is seen that 80 (driver) and 65 (driven) are possible wheels.

COMPOUND GEARS.—When wheels so found are of inconvenient size, a compound train is used, consisting (usually) of two drivers and two driven wheels, the product of the two former and the product of the two latter being in the same ratio as the simple wheels. Thus with 60 and 40 as drivers, and 65 and 30 as driven, we have, $\dfrac{60 \times 40}{65 \times 30} = \dfrac{2400}{1950} = \dfrac{2}{1\cdot 625}$ as before.

With the slide set as above, values convenient for splitting up into suitable wheels are readily obtainable. Thus, $\dfrac{1600}{1300}$; $\dfrac{2400}{1950}$; $\dfrac{4000}{3250}$; $\dfrac{4800}{3900}$ are a few suggestive values which may be readily factorised.

SLIDE RULES FOR SCREW-CUTTING CALCULATIONS.—Special circular and straight slide rules for screw-cutting gear calculations have long been employed. For compound gears these usually entail the use of six scales, two on each of the two slides and two on the stock. The upper scale on the stock may be a scale of threads per inch to be cut, the adjacent scale (on the upper slide) a scale of threads per inch in the guide screw. Setting the guide screw-graduation to the threads to be cut, the lower slide is adjusted until a convenient pair of drivers is found in coincidence on the central pair of scales, while a pair of driven wheels are in coincidence on the two lower scales.

APPENDIX

Some years ago, a slide rule was introduced by which compound gears could be obtained with a single slide. Assuming the set of wheels usually provided—20 to 120 teeth advancing by 5 teeth—the products of 20×25, 20×30, etc., up to 115×120 were calculated. These products were laid out along each of the two lower scales. The upper scales were a scale of threads per inch to be cut and a scale of the threads per inch of various guide screws. Setting the guide screw-graduation to the threads to be cut, any coinciding graduations on the lower scales gave the required pairs of drivers and driven wheels.

FRACTIONAL PITCH CALCULATIONS.—The author has long advocated the use of the slide rule for determining the wheels necessary for cutting fractional pitch threads, and it is gratifying to find its value in this connection is now being appreciated. For the best results a good 20-in. rule is desirable, but with care very close approximations can be found with an accurate 10-in. rule. In any case a magnifying cursor or a hand reading-glass is of great assistance.

Ex.—Find wheels to cut a thread of 0·70909-in. pitch; guide screw, 2 threads per inch.

To 0·70909 on D, set 0·5 (guide screw pitch in inches) on C. To make this setting as accurately as possible, the method described on page 112 may be used. Set 10 on C to about 91 on D, and note that the interval 77–78 on C represents 0·91 of the interval 70–71 on D. Set the cursor to 78 on C and bring 5 to the cursor. The slide is then set so that 5 on C agrees with 7·091 on D.

Inspection of the two scales shows various coinciding factors in the ratio required. The most accurate is seen to be $\frac{55 \text{ on C}}{78 \text{ on D}}$.

These values may be split up into $\frac{55 \times 50}{65 \times 60}$ to form a suitable compound train of gears.

GAUGE POINTS AND SIGNS ON SLIDE RULES.

Many slide rules have the sign $\dfrac{\text{Prod.}}{-1}$ at the right-hand end of the D scale, while on the left is $\dfrac{\text{Quot.}}{+1}$. It is somewhat unfortunate that these signs refer to rules for determining the number of digits in products and quotients, which are used to a considerable extent on the Continent, and conflict with those used in this country. By the Continental method the number of digits in a product is equal to the sum of the digits in the two factors, if the result is obtained on the LEFT *of the first factor;* but if the result is found on the RIGHT of the first factor, it is equal to this sum -1. The sign $\dfrac{\text{Prod.}}{-1}$ at the *right*-hand end of the D scale provides a visible reminder of this rule.

Similarly for division :—The number of digits in a quotient is equal to the number of the digits in the dividend, minus those in the divisor, if the quotient appears on the RIGHT *of the dividend*, and to this difference $+1$, if the quotient appears on the LEFT of the dividend. The sign $\dfrac{\text{Quot.}}{+1}$ at the *left*-hand end of the D scale provides a visible reminder of this rule.

The sign $\overset{+\,|\,-}{\underset{-\,|\,+}{\leftarrow|\rightarrow}}$ found at both ends of the A scale is of general application but of questionable utility. It is assumed to represent a fraction, the vertical line indicating the position of the decimal point. If the number 455 is to be dealt with in a multiplication on the lower scales, we may suppose the decimal point moved two places to the left, giving 4·55, a value which can be actually found on the scale. If we use this value, then to the number of digits in this result, as many must be added as the number of places (two in this case) by which the decimal point was moved. If the point is moved to the right, the number of places must be subtracted. Similarly, in division, if the decimal point in the divisor is moved n places to the left, then n places must be subtracted at the end of the operation; while if the point is moved through n places to the right, then n places must be added. The sign referred to, which, of course, applies to all scales, completely indicates these processes and is submitted as a reminder of the procedure to be followed by those using the method described.

The signs π, c, c', and M are explained in the Section on "Gauge Points," p. 53.

On some rules additional signs are found on the D scale. One, locating the value $\dfrac{180 \times 60}{\pi} = 3437 \cdot 74$ and hence giving the number of minutes in a radian, is marked ϱ'. Another, representing the value $\dfrac{180 \times 60 \times 60}{\pi} = 206265$, and hence giving the number of seconds in a radian is marked ϱ''. A third point, marked ϱ, placed at the value $\dfrac{200 \times 100 \times 100}{\pi} = 636620$, is used when the newer graduation of the circle is employed.

These gauge points are useful when converting angles into circular measure, or *vice versa*, and also for determining the functions of small angles.

A gauge point is sometimes marked at 1146 on the A and B scales. This is known as the "Gunner's Mark," and is used in artillery calculations involving angles of less than 20°, when, for the purpose in view, the tangent and circular measure of the angle may be regarded as equal. For this constant, the angle is taken in minutes, the auxiliary base in feet, and the base in yards. The auxiliary base in feet on B is set to the angle in minutes on A when over 1146 on B is the base in yards on A. The value $\dfrac{1}{1146} = \dfrac{\pi \times 3}{180 \times 60}$.

TABLES AND DATA.

MENSURATION FORMULAE.

Area of a parallelogram = base × height.
Area of rhombus = $\frac{1}{2}$ product of the diagonals.
Area of a triangle = $\frac{1}{2}$ base × perpendicular height.
Area of equilateral triangle = square of side × 0·433.
Area of trapezium = $\frac{1}{2}$ sum of two parallel sides × height.
Area of any right-lined figure of four or more unequal sides is found by dividing it into triangles, finding area of each and adding together.
Area of regular polygon = (1) length of one side × number of sides × radius of inscribed circle; or (2) the sum of the triangular areas into which the figures may be divided.
Circumference of a circle = diameter × 3·1416.
Circumference of circle circumscribing a square = side × 4·443.
Circumference of circle = side of equal square × 3 545.
Length of arc of circle = radius × degrees in arc × 0·01745.
Area of a circle = square of diameter × 0·7854.
Area of sector of a circle = length of arc × $\frac{1}{2}$ radius.
Area of segment of a circle = area of sector − area of triangle.
Side of square of area equal to a circle = diameter × 0·8862.
Diameter of circle equal in area to square = side of square × 1·1284.
Side of square inscribed in circle = diameter of circle × 0·707.
Diameter of circle circumscribing a square = side of square × 1·414.
Area of square = area of inscribed circle × 1·2732.
Area of circle circumscribing square = square of side × 1·5708.
Area of square = area of circumscribing circle × 0·6366.
Area of a parabola = base × $\frac{2}{3}$ height.
Area of an ellipse = major axis × minor axis × 0·7854.
Surface of prism or cylinder = (area of two ends) + (length × perimeter).
Volume of prism or cylinder = area of base × height.
Surface of pyramid or cone = $\frac{1}{2}$(slant height × perimeter of base) + area of base.
Volume of pyramid or cone = $\frac{1}{3}$(area of base × perpendicular height).
Surface of sphere = square of diameter × 3·1416.
Volume of sphere = cube of diameter × 0 5236.
Volume of hexagonal prism = square of side × 2·598 × height.
Volume of paraboloid = $\frac{1}{2}$ volume of circumscribing cylinder.
Volume of ring (circular section) = mean diameter of ring × 2 47 × square of diameter of section.

SPECIFIC GRAVITY AND WEIGHT OF MATERIALS.

METALS.

METAL.	Specific Gravity.	Weight of 1 Cub. Ft (Lb.).	Weight of 1 Cub. In. (Lb.).
Aluminium, Cast	2·56	160	0·0927
Aluminium, Bronze	7·68	475	0·275
Antimony	6·71	418	0·242
Bismuth	9·90	617	0·357
Brass, Cast	8·10	505	0·293
,, Wire	8·548	533	0·309
Copper, Sheet	8·805	549	0·318
,, Wire	8·880	554	0·321
Gold	19·245	1200	0·695
Gun-metal	8·56	534	0·310
Iron, Wrought (mean)	7·698	480	0·278
,, Cast (mean)	7·217	450	0·261
Lead, Milled Sheet	11·418	712	0·412
Manganese	8·012	499	0·289
Mercury	13·596	849	0·491
Nickel, Cast	8·28	516	0·300
Phosphor Bronze, Cast	8·60	536·8	0·310
Platinum	21·522	1342	0·778
Silver	10·505	655	0·380
Steel (mean)	7·852	489·6	0·283
Tin	7·409	462	0·268
Zinc, Sheet	7·20	449	0·260
,, Cast	6·86	428	0·248

MISCELLANEOUS SUBSTANCES.

SUBSTANCE.	Specific Gravity.	Weight of 1 Cub. In. (Lb.).	SUBSTANCE.	Specific Gravity.	Weight of 1 Cub. In. (Lb.).
Asbestos	2·1-2·80	·076-·101	Sand-stone	2·3	·083
Brick	1·90	·069	Slate	2·8	·102
Cement	2·72-3·05	·0984-·109	Wood—		
Clay	2·0	·072	Beech	0·75	·0271
Coal	1·37	·0495	Cork	0·24	·0087
Coke	0·5	·0181	Elm	0·58	·021
Concrete	2·0	·072	Fir	0·56	·0203
Fire-brick	2·30	·083	Oak	·62-·85	·025-·031
Granite	2·5-2·75	·051-·100	Pine	0·47	·017
Graphite	1·8-2·35	·065-·085	Teak	0·80	·029

APPENDIX.

ULTIMATE STRENGTH OF MATERIALS.

MATERIAL.	Tension in lb. per sq. in.	Compression in lb. per sq. in.	Shearing in lb per sq. in.	Modulus of Elasticity in lb. per sq. in.
Cast Iron	11,000 to 30,000	50,000 to 130,000	...	14,000,000 to 23,000,000
,, aver.	16,000	95,000	11,000	...
Wrought Iron	40,000 to 70,000	.	...	26,000,000 to 31,000,000
,, aver.	50,000	50,000	40,000	...
Soft Steel	60,000 to 100,000	...	.	30,000,000 to 36,000,000
Soft Steel - aver.	80,000	70,000	55,000	...
Cast Steel - aver.	120,000	..	..	15,000,000 to 17,000,000
Copper, Cast -	19,000	58,000	...	...
,, Wrought -	34,000	...	...	16,000,000
Brass, Cast -	18,000	10,500	...	9,170,000
Gun Metal	34,000	...	.	11,500,000
Phosphor Bronze	58,000	...	43,000	13,500,000
Wood, Ash	17,000	9,300	1,400	.
,, Beech	16,000	8,500	...	..
,, Pine	11,000	6,000	650	1,400,000
,, Oak	15,000	10,000	2,300	1,500,000
Leather - -	4,200	.	..	25,000

POWERS, ROOTS, ETC., OF USEFUL FACTORS.

n	$\dfrac{1}{n}$	n^2	n^3	$\sqrt{n}$	$\dfrac{1}{\sqrt{n}}$	$\sqrt[3]{n}$	$\dfrac{1}{\sqrt[3]{n}}$
$\pi = 3.142$	0.318	9.870	31.006	1.772	0.564	1.465	0.683
$2\pi = 6.283$	0.159	39.478	248.050	2.507	0.399	1.845	0.542
$\dfrac{\pi}{2} = 1.571$	0.637	2.467	3.878	1.253	0.798	1.162	0.860
$\dfrac{\pi}{3} = 1.047$	0.955	1.097	1.148	1.023	0.977	1.016	0.985
$\dfrac{4}{3}\pi = 4.189$	0.239	17.546	73.496	2.047	0.489	1.612	0.622
$\dfrac{\pi}{4} = 0.785$	1.274	0.617	0.484	0.886	1.128	0.923	1.084
$\dfrac{\pi}{6} = 0.524$	1.910	0.274	0.144	0.724	1.382	0.806	1.241
$\pi^2 = 9.870$	0.101	97.409	961.390	3.142	0.318	2.145	0.466
$\pi^3 = 31.006$	0.032	961.390	29,809.910	5.568	1.796	3.142	0.318
$\dfrac{\pi}{32} = 0.098$	10.186	0.0095	0.001	0.313	3.192	0.461	2.168
$g = 32.2$	0.031	1036.84	33,386.24	5.674	0.176	3.181	0.314
$2g = 64.4$	0.015	4147.36	267,090	8.025	0.125	4.007	0.249

APPENDIX.

HYDRAULIC EQUIVALENTS.

1 foot head = 0 434 lb. per square inch.
1 lb. per square inch = 2 31 ft. head
1 imperial gallon = 277·274 cubic inches.
1 imperial gallon = 0·16045 cubic foot.
1 imperial gallon = 10 lb.
1 cubic foot of water = 62·32 lb. = 6·232 imperial gallons.
1 cubic foot of sea water = 64 00 lb.
1 cubic inch of water = 0·03616 lb.
1 cubic inch of sea water = 0·037037 lb.
1 cylindrical foot of water = 48 96 lb.
1 cylindrical inch of water = 0·0284 lb.
A column of water 12 in. long 1 in. square = 0·434 lb.
A column of water 12 in. long 1 in. diameter = 0·340 lb.
Capacity of a 12 in cube = 6 232 gallons.
Capacity of a 1 in. square 1 ft. long = 0 0434 gallon.
Capacity of a 1 ft. diameter 1 ft. long = 4·896 gallons.
Capacity of a cylinder 1 in. diameter 1 ft. long = 0·034 gallon.
Capacity of a cylindrical inch = 0 002832 gallon.
Capacity of a cubic inch = 0·003606 gallon.
Capacity of a sphere 12 in. diameter = 3·263 gallons.
Capacity of a sphere 1 in. diameter = 0·00188 gallon.
1 imperial gallon = 1·2 United States gallon.
1 imperial gallon = 4·543 litres of water.
1 United States gallon = 231·0 cubic inches.
1 United States gallon = 0 83 imperial gallon.
1 United States gallon = 3·8 litres of water.
1 cubic foot of water = 7·476 United States gallons.
1 cubic foot of water = 28·375 litres of water.
1 litre of water = 0 22 imperial gallon.
1 litre of water = 0·264 United States gallon.
1 litre of water = 61 0 cubic inches.
1 litre of water = 0·0353 cubic foot.

EQUIVALENTS OF POUNDS AVOIRDUPOIS.

	10	100	1000	10,000	100,000
	qr. lb	cwt. qr. lb	ton cwt. qr. lb.	ton cwt. qr. lb.	ton cwt qr lb
1	0 10	0 3 16	0 8 3 20	4 9 1 4	44 12 3 12
2	0 20	1 3 4	0 17 3 12	8 18 2 8	89 5 2 24
3	1 2	2 2 20	1 6 3 4	13 7 3 12	133 18 2 8
4	1 12	3 2 8	1 15 2 24	17 17 0 16	178 11 1 20
5	1 22	4 1 24	2 4 2 16	22 6 1 20	223 4 1 4
6	2 4	5 1 12	2 13 2 8	26 15 2 24	267 17 0 16
7	2 14	6 1 0	3 2 2 0	31 5 0 0	312 10 0 0
8	2 24	7 0 16	3 11 1 20	35 14 1 4	357 2 3 12
9	3 6	8 0 4	4 0 1 12	40 3 2 8	401 15 2 24

APPENDIX.

TRIGONOMETRICAL FUNCTIONS.

RIGHT-ANGLED TRIANGLES.

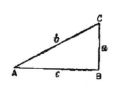

$$\text{Sin. } A = \frac{a}{b} \qquad \text{Sec. } A = \frac{b}{c} \qquad \text{Tan. } A = \frac{a}{c}$$

$$\text{Cos. } A = \frac{c}{b} \qquad \text{Cosec. } A = \frac{b}{a} \qquad \text{Cotan. } A = \frac{c}{a}$$

$$\text{Versin. } A = \frac{b-c}{b} \qquad \text{Coversin } A = \frac{b-a}{b}$$

Given.	Required.	Formulæ.		
a, b	A, C, c	$\text{Sin. } A = \frac{a}{b}$	$\text{Cos. } C = \frac{a}{b}$	$c = \sqrt{(b+a)(b-a)}$
a, c	A, C, b	$\text{Tan } A = \frac{a}{c}$	$\text{Cotan. } B = \frac{a}{c}$	$b = \sqrt{(a^2 + c^2)}$
A, a	C, c, b	$C = 90° - A$	$c = a \times \text{Cotan. } A$	$b = \frac{a}{\text{Sin. } A}$
A, b	C, a, c	$C = 90° - A$	$a = b \times \text{Sin. } A$	$c = b \times \text{Cos. } A$
A, c	C, a, b	$C = 90° - A$	$a = c \times \text{Tan. } A$	$b = \frac{c}{\text{Cos. } A}$

OBLIQUE-ANGLED TRIANGLES.

$s = \frac{1}{2}(a+b+c)$

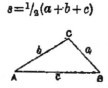

Given.	Formulæ.
A, B, C, a A, b, c a, b, c	$\text{Area} = \begin{cases} (a^2 \times \text{Sin. } B \times \text{Sin. } C) \div 2 \text{ Sin. } A \\ \frac{1}{2}(c \times b \times \text{Sin. } A) \\ \sqrt{s(s-a)(s-b)(s-c)} \end{cases}$

Given.	Required.	Formulæ.
A, C, a	c	$c = a \dfrac{\text{Sin. } C}{\text{Sin. } A}$
A, a, c	C	$\text{Sin. } C = \dfrac{c \text{ Sin. } A}{a}$
a, c, B	A	$\text{Tan. } A = \dfrac{a \text{ Sin. } B}{c - a \text{ Cos. } B}$
a, b, c	A	$\begin{cases} \text{Sin. } \frac{1}{2}A = \sqrt{\dfrac{(s-b)(s-c)}{b \times c}} \\ \text{Cos. } \frac{1}{2}A = \sqrt{\dfrac{s(s-a)}{b \times c}}; \ \text{Tan. } \frac{1}{2}A = \sqrt{\dfrac{(s-b)(s-c)}{s(s-a)}} \end{cases}$

COMPOUND ANGLES

$\text{Sin. } (A+B) = \text{Sin. } A \text{ Cos. } B + \text{Cos. } A \text{ Sin. } B$
$\text{Sin. } (A-B) = \text{Sin. } A \text{ Cos. } B - \text{Cos. } A \text{ Sin. } B$
$\text{Cos. } (A+B) = \text{Cos. } A \text{ Cos. } B - \text{Sin. } A \text{ Sin. } B$
$\text{Cos. } (A-B) = \text{Cos. } A \text{ Cos. } B + \text{Sin. } A \text{ Sin. } B$

$\text{Tan. } (A+B) = \dfrac{\text{Tan. } A + \text{Tan. } B}{1 - \text{Tan. } A \text{ Tan. } B}$
$\text{Tan. } (A-B) = \dfrac{\text{Tan. } A - \text{Tan. } B}{1 + \text{Tan. } A \text{ Tan. } B}$

SLIDE RULE DATA SLIPS, COMPILED BY C. N. PICKWORTH, WH.SC.

(It is suggested that this page be removed by cutting through the above line, and selected portions of the Sectional Data Slips attached to the back of the Slide Rule.)

$\frac{1}{32}$	0·03125	$1\frac{1}{32}$	0·34375
$\frac{1}{16}$	0·0625	$\frac{3}{8}$	0·375
$\frac{3}{32}$	0·09375	$1\frac{3}{32}$	0·40625
$\frac{1}{8}$	0·125	$\frac{7}{16}$	0·4375
$\frac{5}{32}$	0·15625	$1\frac{5}{32}$	0·46875
$\frac{3}{16}$	0·1875	$\frac{1}{2}$	0·5
$\frac{7}{32}$	0·21875	$1\frac{7}{32}$	0·53125
$\frac{1}{4}$	0·25	$\frac{9}{16}$	0·5625
$\frac{9}{32}$	0·28125	$1\frac{9}{32}$	0·59375
$\frac{5}{16}$	0·3125	$\frac{5}{8}$	0·625
		$1\frac{11}{32}$	0·65625

Circ. of circle = 3·1416 d.
Area ,, = 0·7854 d^2.
Sq. eq. area to cir., $s = 0.886\, d$.
Circle eq. to sq., $d = 1.128\, s$.
Sq inscbd. in circ., $s = 0.707\, d$.
Circsb. circ. of sq., $d = 1.414\, s$.
Area of ellipse = 0·7854 $a \times b$.
Surface of sphere = 3·1416 d^2.
Volume ,, = 0·5236 d^3.
,, cone = 0·2618 $d^2 h$.

Radian = 180°/π = 57·29 deg.
Base of nat. or hyp. log. = e = 2·7183.
Nat. or hyp. log ÷ com. log. × 2·3026.
g (at London) 32·18 ft. per sec., per sec.
Abs. temp = deg. F. + 461° = deg. C + 274°.
C.° = 5/9 (F.° − 32°); F.° = 9/5 C.° + 32°.
Cal. pr.—Ther. units per lb.: Coal, 14,300; petrol'm, 20,000, coal gas per cu. ft., 700.
Sp. heat:—Wt., iron, 0·1138; C.I. 0·1298, copper, brass, 0·095; lead, 0·0314.

Inch = 25·4 mil'metres, mil'metre = 0·03937 in.
Foot = 0·3048 metres; metre = 3·2809 feet
Yard = 0·91438 metre; metre = 1·0936 yards.
Mile = 1·6093 kilomtrs.; kilomtr. = 0·6213 mile.
Sq. in. = 6·4513 sq. cm.; sq. cm. = 0·155 sq. in.
Sq. ft. = 9·29 sq. decmtr.; sq. decmtr. = 0·1076 sq. ft.
Sq. yd. = 0·836 sq. metre; sq. metre = 1·196 sq. yds
Sq. ml. = 258·9 hectares; hectare = 0·00386 sq. ml
Cu. in. = 16·386 c. cm.; c. cm. = 0·06102 cu. in.
Cu. ft. = 0·0283 c.metre; c.metre = 35·316 cu. ft.

Grain = 0·0648 gramme, gram. = 15·43 grs.
Ounce = 28·35 grams; ,, = 0·03527 oz
Pound = 0·4556 kilogm.; kilogm. = 2·204 lb.
Ton = 1·016 tonnes; tonne = 0·9842 ton.
Mile per hr. = 1·466 ft. or 44·7 cm., per sec
Lb. per cu. in. = 0·0276 kilogram per cu. cm
Kilogram per cu cm. = 36·125 lb per cu in
Lb. per cu. ft. = 16·019 kilog. per cu. mtre.
Grain per gall. = 0·01426 gramme per litre,
Gramme per litre = 70·116 grains per gall.

Lb. per sq. in. = 2·31 ft. water = 2·04 in. mercury = 0·0703 kilo per sq. cm.
Atmoephere = 14·7 lb per sq. in. = 33·94 ft. water = 1·0335 ,, ,, ,,
Ft. hd. water = 0·4331 lb. per sq. in. = 62·351 lb. per sq. ft. = 0·0304 ,,
Cub. ft. of water = 62·35 lb. = 0·0278 ton = 28·315 litres = 7·43 U'S. galls.
Gall (Imp.) = 277·27 cu in = 0·1604 cu. ft. = 10 lb. water = 4·544 litres.
Litre = 1·76 pints = 0·22 gall. = 61 cu. in. = 0·0353 cu. ft. = 0·264 U.S gall.
Horse-power = 33,000 ft.-lb. per min. = 0·746 kilowatt = 42·4 heat unite per min.
Heat unit = 778 ft.-lb. = 1055 watt-sec. = 107·5 kilogrammetres = 0·252 calorie.
Foot-pound = 0·00129 heat unit = 1·36 joules = 0·1383 kilogrammetres.
Kilowatt = 1·34 H.P. = 44,240 ft.-lb. per min. = 2412 heat units per hour.

Weight of Metals {	Cub. In.	Cub. Ft.	12 Cu. In.
Wt., iron	0·277	480	3·33
Cast ,,	0·260	450	3·12
Steel ,,	0·283	490	3·40
Copper	0·318	550	3·82
Brass	0·300	520	3·61
Zinc	0·248	430	2·98
Alumin'm	0·096	168	1·16
Lead	0·411	710	4·93

	Ultimate Strength }	Lb. per Sq. In.	
		Tens'n	Comp'n
Wt., iron		50,000	50,000
Cast ,,		16,000	95,000
Steel ,,		80,000	70,000
Copper		21,000	50,000
Brass		18,000	10,500
Lead		2,500	7,000
Pine		11,000	6,000
Oak		15,000	10,000

ADVERTISEMENTS.

LOGARITHMS FOR BEGINNERS

For a full and intelligent appreciation of the Slide Rule and its various applications an elementary knowledge of logarithms is necessary. All that is required will be found in this little work, which gives a simple, detailed and practical explanation of logarithms and their uses, particular care having been taken to elucidate all difficult points by the aid of a number of worked examples

Seventh Edition.   1s. 8d. Post Free.

POWER COMPUTER
FOR
STEAM, GAS, AND OIL ENGINES, Etc.

Gives The Indicated Horse-Power of Steam, Gas, and Oil Engines—The Brake Horse-Power of Steam, Gas, and Oil Engines—The Size of Engine Necessary to Develop any Given Power—The Mechanical Efficiency of an Engine—The Ratio of Compound Engine Cylinders—The Piston Speed of an Engine—The Delivery of Pumps with any Efficiency—The Horse-Power of Belting—The Rim Speeds of Wheels, Speeds of Ropes, Belts, etc.—Speed Ratios of Pulleys, Gearing, etc. Pocket size, in neat case, with instructions and examples

Post Free, 7s. 6d. net.

C. N. PICKWORTH, Withington, Manchester

W. P. THOMPSON, F.C.S., M.I.Mech.E., F.I.C.P.A	**G. C. DYMOND,** M.I.Mech.E., F.I.C.P.A

W. P. THOMPSON & Co.,
12 CHURCH STREET, LIVERPOOL,
CHARTERED PATENT AGENTS.

H. E. POTTS, M.Sc., Hon. Chem., F.I.C.P.A	**J. V. ARMSTRONG,** M.Text.I., F.I.C.P.A

W. H. BEESTON, R.P.A.

BRITISH SLIDE RULES

for all

ARTS and INDUSTRIES

including

LOG-O-LOG

DR YOKOTA'S

SURVEYORS'

WIRELESS

GUNNERY

ELECTRICAL RULES, Etc.

SEND FOR LIST 55

MADE BY—

John Davis & Son (Derby), Ltd.

ALL SAINTS' WORKS, DERBY

K & E Slide Rules

are constantly growing in popularity, and they can now be obtained from the leading houses in our line throughout the United Kingdom.

We manufacture a complete line of **ENGINE-DIVIDED SLIDE RULES,** and call special attention to our Patent Adjustment, ensuring smooth working of the Slide; also to our new "Frameless" Indicator, which hides no figures on the Rule.

THACHER'S CALCULATING INSTRUMENT, for solving problems in multiplication, division, or combinations of the two; has upwards of 33,000 divisions. Results can be obtained to the fourth and usually to the fifth place of figures with a surprising degree of accuracy.

We also make
ALL METAL, CIRCULAR, STADIA, CHEMISTS', ELECTRICAL, and OTHER SPECIAL SLIDE RULES

DESCRIPTIVE CIRCULARS ON REQUEST

KEUFFEL & ESSER CO.

127 Fulton St., NEW YORK   General Office and Factories, HOBOKEN, N.J.

CHICAGO - ST. LOUIS - SAN FRANCISCO - MONTREAL

DRAWING MATERIALS
MATHEMATICAL and SURVEYING INSTRUMENTS
MEASURING TAPES

ADVERTISEMENTS

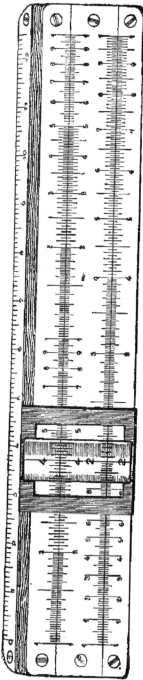

6 in. Standard with magnifying Cursor complete in pocket case, 5/-

NORTON & GREGORY
LTD.

Head Office
CASTLE LANE, WESTMINSTER, LONDON, S.W. 1

Branches
71 QUEEN STREET, GLASGOW.
PHOENIX HOUSE, QUEEN STREET and SANDHILL, NEWCASTLE-ON-TYNE.

SLIDE RULES in Stock, from 17/6 to 27/6

Special Quotations to the Trade for Quantities

For particulars of Surveying, Measuring and Mathematical Instruments, Appliances and Material of all kinds for the Drawing Office, write to the Head Office

NORTON & GREGORY, LTD.,
London.

"DIAMOND"
DRAWING INSTRUMENTS
Manufactured at our London Works.

CENTRE SCREW SPRING BOW HALF SET.

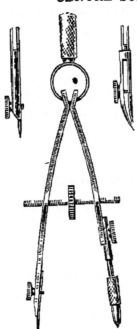

4 inch Spring Bow Half Set centre screw adjustment, with interchangeable needle, pen, and pencil points   Price 17/6

The Centre Screw Spring Bow Half Set of Compasses, as illustrated, possesses the advantage of COMBINING IN ONE INSTRUMENT THE SET OF THREE SEPARATE SPRING BOWS hitherto in use, while the centre screw makes for ease and accuracy of manipulation, at the same time providing a radius of over 2 inches, or double that of the old pattern.

This instrument is less expensive than the set of 3 bows, while considerbly stronger in construction

The fixed needle point is shouldered

This illustration is given as an indication of the various Drawing Instruments manufactured by us

Illustrated Booklet giving full particulars and prices of other Instruments and Cases of Instruments sent on application.

Specially arranged Sets of Instruments made for Colleges, Schools, Technical Institutes

Estimates submitted on Application.

Write to our Head Office:
CASTLE LANE, WESTMINSTER, LONDON, S.W.I.

DRAWING AND SURVEYING INSTRUMENTS

SLIDE RULES FOR ENGINEERS

A. G. THORNTON Ltd.
Paragon Works
2 King St. West
MANCHESTER

ACCURATE SECTIONAL PAPERS AND CLOTHS

D 1916 Illustrated Catalogue, just published, in two editions; Drawing Office (448 pages); Draughtsman's (160 pages): the most complete Catalogues in the trade.

CONTRACTORS TO H.M. WAR OFFICE AND ADMIRALTY
Manufacturers also of Drawing Materials and Drawing Office Stationery.

(ALSO AT MINERVA WORKS AND ALBERT MILLS, MANCHESTER.)

MATHEMATICAL INSTRUMENTS

SURVEYING INSTRUMENTS

SLIDE RULES
For Students and Engineers

MANNHEIM, POLYPHASE, DUPLEX, ELECTRICAL, LOG=LOG, AND CALCULEX

J. H. STEWARD LTD.
Scientific Instrument Makers

406 STRAND, and 457 WEST STRAND
LONDON, W.C. 2

A True Friend and Trusty Guide

THE 'HALDEN CALCULEX'

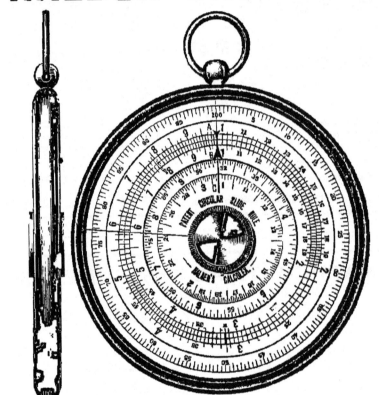

ACTUAL SIZE   **BRITISH MADE**

The handiest and most perfect form of Slide Rule. Does all that can be done with a straight rule. Complete in Case, with book of instructions, **27/6** post free.

J. HALDEN & CO., LTD., 8 ALBERT SQUARE MANCHESTER

Depots—London, Newcastle-on-Tyne, Birmingham, Glasgow, and Leeds

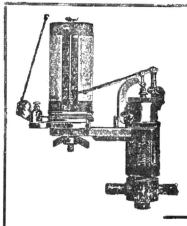

ENGINEERING, SURVEYING
AND
MATHEMATICAL INSTRUMENTS,
ETC.

SLIDE RULES.

JOSEPH CASARTELLI & SON,
43 MARKET STREET, MANCHESTER.

Tel. No. 2958 City. Established 1790.

ROPE DRIVING
Is the most EFFICIENT and most ECONOMICAL METHOD of Power Transmission.

The LAMBETH Cotton Driving Rope
Is the most EFFICIENT and most ECONOMICAL ROPE for Power Transmission.

Made 4 Strand or 3 Strand.

SPECIAL FEATURES:
LESS STRETCH THAN ANY OTHER ROPE.
MORE PLIABLE THAN ANY OTHER ROPE.
GREATER DRIVING POWER THAN ANY OTHER ROPE.

THOMAS HART LTD., Lambeth Works, BLACKBURN.

CPSIA information can be obtained
at www.ICGtesting.com
Printed in the USA
BVOW07s0227031017
496562BV00008B/110/P